SENIOR MANAGEMENT—
THE DYNAMICS
OF EFFECTIVENESS

SENIOR MANAGEMENT—
THE DYNAMICS
OF EFFECTIVENESS

Sushila Singhal

Sage Publications
New Delhi • Thousand Oaks • London

To Gauri Shankar, Namita, Renu and Mridu

First published in 1994 by

Sage Publications India Pvt Ltd
M-32, Greater Kailash Market I
New Delhi 110048.

Sage Publications Inc		**Sage Publications Ltd**
2455 Teller Road		6, Bonhill Street
Thousand Oaks, California 91320		London EC2A 4PU

Published by Tejeshwar Singh for Sage Publications India Pvt Ltd, laser typeset by Print Line, Delhi and printed at Chaman Enterprises, Delhi.

Library of Congress Cataloging-in-Publication Data

Singhal, Sushila
    Senior Management: the dynamics of effectiveness / Sushila Singhal
        p.   cm.
    Includes bibliographical references and index.
    1. Executive ability. 2. Management. I. Title.
    HD38.2.S56   1994   658.4′ 093—dc20   94–15770

ISBN: 81-7036-408-6 (India-Hb) 0-8039-9180-0 (US-Hb)
       81-7036-409-4 (India-Pb) 0-8039-9181-9 (US-Pb)

CONTENTS

LIST OF TABLES

FOREWORD

I am very happy to introduce this book to the expert and user community. Professor Sushila Singhal writes on managerial perceptions and the dynamics of their effectiveness. This is a period of great change for the Indian corporate sector and she analyzes in considerable detail the problems of managerial perceptions. Her findings on the lack of self-perception in senior managers are interesting. The whole question of the perception of the environment for business in a period of globalization and liberalization is critical. Managerial perceptions of political interference and their role in corporate strategies is a peculiar feature of the life of Indian management. Finally, Professor Singhal's comments on the great Indian penchant to solve problems with 'paper' approvals make a telling impact. All in all this is a thoroughly enjoyable book which can be read with great profit.

2 March, 1994

Y.K. Alagh
Vice-Chancellor
Jawaharlal Nehru University
New Delhi

PREFACE

Over the last two decades the public sector has been a target of constant criticism from all sections of society, including bureaucrats and politicians. Not only are the problems difficult to comprehend, but the solutions offered are irrelevant and out of context. Often such indulgence seems like a pastime and life goes on as usual. Effectiveness is a dynamic concept whether it is used to evaluate individuals or organizations. It is an evolving process and is relative to time, space and goal orientations. Individuals judged effective today may or may not be considered so later, as their position in the matrix of variables may undergo changes. It is even more true of groups and organizations, as their effectiveness is contingent on numerous factors beyond their control, such as the context of international markets, socio-political environment, management at the top, resource availability and non-occurrence of the expected or the planned. This makes the task of selecting appropriate and relevant indicators difficult; particularly so in the context of the public sector where most corporations are large, have contradictory goals and policies, and are under multiple controls.

In the present investigation, I have made persistent efforts to cope with the stipulated tasks of operationalizing clearly the managers' effectiveness, of choosing appropriate indicators and tools, and of arriving at certain conclusions, however tentative. I have tried to link the findings with theory and policy prescriptions guiding/regulating the public sector as people are hopeful that this sector will accelerate the economic development of the country. The choice of tools and method of analysis reflect the bias of my training in psychology, but I have tried to make the text adequately comprehensive, of interest to researchers in sister disciplines and for practicing managers. It is hoped that the book will be found equally useful and informative by teachers, researchers and managers who are concerned about understanding, analysing and finding solutions to the problems of management in different types of corporations. Its focus is on the effectiveness of senior and top-level managers. The presentation is arranged around specific themes designed to indicate what is generally understood.

The book is organized in the form of ten chapters. Chapter I introduces the problem of managerial effectiveness in the corporate world which has an interface with the larger society. Numerous theoretical models have been evaluated and a case is made for an integrative framework to examine managerial effectiveness. In Chapter 2 some of the specific issues of corporate management are identified through an extensive and intensive search and the strategy of the investigation has been spelled out. Although the major focus of the investigation has been on the public sector, a comparative group from the private sector is included. Only the senior and top-level managers constitute the sample as they have the major responsibility for the smooth running of corporate operations and only a few researchers have reported on their problems, perceptions and achievements. Chapters 3 to 8 present quantitative analyses of psychological dispositions of managers, their time manangement, goal achievement, role perceptions, confidence and professional commitment. These contain some very revealing findings which are integrated into existing theory, evidence and practices. Chapter 9 reports on the qualitative data obtained through interviews, discussions, anecdotes, handouts etc. This contributes to the existing information about the functioning of the corporate world, the policies in practice, and the issues that crave for immediate attention, if the industrial sector has to yield returns to sustain it even at the minimal level. Chapter 10 includes a summary of the findings and the implications of these findings from the point of view of theory and policy, inclusive of the New Industrial Policy prescriptions.

The book is based on the research project 'Socio-Organizational and Personal Determinants of Managerial Effectiveness.' This research project was sanctioned during my tenure as Professor at the Sri Ram Centre for Industrial Relations and Human Resources, New Delhi, on lien from the Jawaharlal Nehru University (JNU), New Delhi. As soon as the project was launched, it had to be transferred to the JNU. The implementation of the project and the submission of the report were delayed (much against my liking) because of numerous problems—technical and administrative. To cut a long story short, during the period sanctioned by the Indian Council for Social Science

Research, only the data could be collected. A significant part of the project work was completed afterwards and along with my full-time job. I am extremely pleased to have seen it to its fruition.

I thank the Indian Council for Social Science Research, New Delhi, for the grant that made the research project possible, although a major part of the work had to be done in my own time as a faculty member at JNU. I am extremely grateful to our Vice-Chancellor, Professor Y.K. Alagh, for spending his valuable time in writing the foreword to the book. I am greatly indebted to the late Mr. Arun Joshi, who as Executive Director of the Shri Ram Centre for Industrial Relations and Human Resource Management, New Delhi, shared my preconceptions and ideas and made the formulation of the proposal possible. I am also deeply grateful to the managements of the corporations which participated in this venture and provided the material to construct the body and soul of this book. It was a pleasure meeting most of them, even though I had to wait for long periods of time and had to make several requests before I could interview them. I am thankful to the various research investigators who worked for different time periods, the typists who shared the work of putting my repeated drafts on the word processor, and last but not the least, to my family members for their constant moral support.

August 1993   **Sushila Singhal**

1

INTRODUCTION: MANAGERS AND EFFECTIVENESS

Centrality of Managers

Senior managers are key actors in the corporate world. What they do, how they do it, and why they do it should aptly reflect the objectives, plans, policies and organizational processes of a corporation, and its unique relationship with other organizations and with the larger society. These questions are useful in defining not only their corporate and personal agenda, but also their concerns, roles and obligations, perceptions, strategies and techniques, motivation and commitment.

Structurally, senior managers constitute the most visible core group in the organizations. They are at the helm of affairs and represent a distinct group in terms of their social psychological orientations, skills, competence, professionalism and efficiency. They have the responsibility of translating the policies and decisions into programmes of action and making these comprehensible to their juniors. Functionally, they have the power to set corporate-level goals, to choose matching processes, technology and activities, and to identify the nature of physical and human resource requirements. The achievement of corporate goals is contingent upon them and at the same time depends on the cooperation, involvement and mutual support of participants at all levels. Managers have an interface of roles with policymakers, bureaucrats, corporate chiefs and subordinate managerial and supervisory cadres. Their professional links, role perceptions and job attitudes encompass relationships with persons at a number of levels, both above and below. Such an interface, though difficult to assess directly, is relevant and necessary in the understanding and analysis of the dynamics of managerial effectiveness. Further, differences in corporate settings and mandates may make diverse provisions and demands on managers, deserving inclusion in assessments of effectiveness.

Functions of Management

The functions of management are necessarily diverse and include planning, finance, human resource development, production, marketing, sales, management of information systems etc. They may be differentially challenging and competitive in different corporations in the same country, and in different countries, depending on models of national economy and levels of development. There is greater emphasis on clear operational goals and specifications in developed countries. The reverse is the case in developing and less developed countries. Although corporations are formal organizations, in these countries the guidelines are not fully formalized and clearcut. Practices are entrenched in informality. This makes the functions of management in developing countries relatively more complex and often vague. Managers in these countries are compelled to introduce imported technologies, modes of production and services in socio-cultural conditions to which they are least suitable. They have to shoulder the responsibilities of performing the strategic tasks of choosing an appropriate organizational design, of finding a good fit between the organizational design and the socio-cultural context, setting the standards of operation and achieving inter-unit coordination.

Managers are called upon to discharge multiple functions and in the process to effectively relate to numerous individuals and agencies—formal, informal, local, regional, national and foreign. Some of these are: government officials, bureaucrats, planners, local residents and groups, financial agencies, supply and procurement groups, law enforcing agencies, educational agencies, sister corporations, and foreign agencies. Corporate success depends on the smooth, efficient and well-coordinated functioning of the units and the individual members, but this requires a herculean effort to achieve. Managers have to manage to do the right things and also to try to do things right.

Different corporations within a country are guided by basic planning models and policy considerations, but all corporations do not translate these into action in a similar manner. Even within the same sector all corporations do not perform at the same level. In fact, managers in charge of different units tend to react differently to similar policy prescriptions and organizational demands, resulting in varying inter-manager and inter-unit differences. This makes organizational as well as individual difference dimensions equally relevant in the understanding and analysis of the perceptions, experiences, practices and performance of managers.

The Organizational Difference Dimension

It has been advocated that organizational attributes are the source of variance in organizational effectiveness. These are characterized as efficiency and maximization of returns (Katz and Kahn, 1966); adaptability, sense of identity and capacity to test reality (Bennis, 1966); the ability of an organization to mobilize its centres of power for action, production and adaptation (Mott, 1972); overall performance, productivity, employee satisfaction, profit and withdrawal based on turnover/ absenteeism (Campbell, 1977); effective dealing of the external environment to secure the resources needed for the organization (Steers, 1975); and profit maximization and managerial job behaviour (Morse and Wagner, 1978). A number of models have been proposed that encompass the total meaning of organizational effectiveness. Prominent among these are the goal model (Bluedorn, 1980; Price, 1972); the system resource model (Yuchtman and Seashore, 1967); the internal processes or maintenance model (Bennis, 1966); the strategic constituencies model (Connolly, Conlon and Deutch, 1980; Keeley. 1978; Pfeffer and Salancik, 1978); and the legitimacy model (Miles and Cameron, 1982; Zammuto, 1982). The models differ in terms of assumptions, foci and powers of explanation. The choice of an appropriate model should depend on the type of organization studied, its complexity, and its relevance in the environment and in the current industrial policy.

Campbell (1977) has viewed organizational effectiveness as the degree to which the 'end' objectives of organizations are accomplished, subject to certain constraints. Pennings and Goodman (1977) have integrated the various theories of organizational effectiveness and have proposed a new conceptual framework in which organizations may be effective, if relevant constraints are satisfied, and if organizational results approximate or exceed a set of referents for multiple goals. It has been noted by Cameron (1978) that organizational effectiveness may be typified as mutable (composed of different criteria at different stages of life), comprehensive (inclusive of multiple dimensions), divergent (of different constituents), transpositive (capable of altering relevant criteria to match the level of analysis), and complex (having dimensions of non-parsimonious relationships). In the context of the public sector in India, Singh (1978) and Chaturvedi (1980) have advocated the use of multiple perspectives in assessing the effectiveness of corporations, each corresponding to a distinctive view of the organization (such as a rational, purposive, and survival-oriented system). It is suggested that the focus should be on the efficacy of an organization vis-à-vis its acquisition of inputs, the process of transformation of inputs, the disposition of outputs and the organization's ability to respond to the feedback from the environment.

Miles (1980) has proposed a convergence model called the 'ecology model' in which organizational effectiveness has been defined as 'the ability of the organization to minimally satisfy the expectations of its strategic constituencies'. He has·conceived of organizational effectiveness not as a one-shot affair, but as 'an ongoing process'. Van de Ven and Ferry (1980) have suggested that the question of 'organizational effectiveness from a person's perspective' should be taken into account and thus have emphasized 'user' values. According to Peters and Waterman (1982) every excellent company is clear about what it stands on, and takes the process of forming values quite seriously, thereby contributing to its effectiveness. Cummings (1983) has compared the different perspectives of organizational effectiveness and has observed that under competitive conditions, the proposition of enhancing effectiveness centres on increasing the ratio of outputs to inputs. The consequent effectiveness strategies should thus focus on either increasing the fit between persons and jobs, and/or increasing the focus and persistence of motivation of individuals through the more intelligent design of reward systems, tasks and the organizational units (Schmidt, Hunter, McKenzie and Muldrow, 1979).

Organizational effectiveness has also been viewed as a socially constructed, abstract notion carried about in the heads of organizational theorists and researchers (Quinn and Rohrbaugh, 1983). They have used models by Scott (1977), Seashore (1979) and Cameron (1979) to map various effectiveness constructs onto a 'spatial model'. Cameron and Whetten (1983) have stated that no single approach to effectiveness is inherently superior to any other as all these are multiple conceptions of organizations and unbounded construct space, and suffer from the absence of consensual criteria. The issue of effectiveness causality can thus be approached from a number of directions. Some of the emerging directions are organizational culture (Quinn and Rohrbaugh, 1983; Martin, Sitkin and Boehm, 1984); employee loyalty (Zahra, 1984; Reichers, 1985); executive leadership (Miller, Toulouse and Belanger, 1985); life cycle stage (Cameron, 1984; Quinn and McGrath, 1984); virtual positions within organizations (Mackenzie, 1986); attributes of information processing and decision-making (Huber and McDaniel, 1986a, 1986b) and organizational designs (Daft and Lengel, 1986). Cameron (1986a) has examined the issues of consensus and conflict in the conceptions of organizational effectiveness, and has observed that often the criteria of effectiveness are of a paradoxical nature, and yet need to be taken into account. There is so much confusion and disagreement about the concept of effectiveness that it fails to provide clear guidelines for future research.

Lewin and Minton (1986) have reviewed the research related to the components of contingency behaviour theory of organizational effectiveness. They have proposed the use of the strategy of engineering organizational effectiveness by involving a partnership between practitioners and researchers. The strategic human resource management model of organizational effectiveness has been found useful by Evans (1986), since it takes into account: (a) the internal focus—equity and human relations; (b) the external focus—competitive performance; (c) the organizational environment boundary focus—innovation and flexibility; and (d) the inner unit focus—corporate integration. Further, if effectiveness is viewed as the outcome of a variety of decisions taken by one or more groups of organizational actors–elites or coalitions in the context of bounded rationalities and environmental and structural constraints, one can make use of even a biographical approach (Kimberly and Rottman, 1987) to complement the quantitative analysis.

The Individual Difference Dimension

Theorists who focus on the individual difference dimension have used individual difference as the source of behaviour, be it performance, commitment, involvement or anything else. The assumption has been that in any corporation the task and the technology used may interact with the attributes of the members, and give rise to different perceptions and responses to organizational contingencies. In the literature reviewed, individual differences have been investigated by a variety of approaches managers have used, such as the role approach, the goal approach, the developmental approach, the professional commitment approach, the hierarchical approach and the integrative approach. These are briefly examined below:

The Role Approach

The role approach theorists consider the performance of roles by managers as central to their analysis. It has been argued that managers who perform their roles efficiently as individuals, would also be effective at the organizational level. If managers are able to understand clearly what is expected of them in encountering the organizational contingencies, they can continually compare, evaluate and monitor their own roles vis-à-vis the prototype role sets and the roles of others, and take the necessary steps to enhance their effectiveness. Managerial roles have been categorized by Mintzberg (1973) into three types: interpersonal, informational and decisional. Managers, who can structure people and resources to extract the relevant information for decision-making, can play their roles efficiently and also facilitate organizational effectiveness. McDonnell (1974) has included intelligent compromise as an essential element in the decision-making role of managers. A set of managerial roles has been found implicit in the identification of six dimensions of managerial effectiveness by Morse and Wagner (1978). These are: (a) managing the organizational environment and its resources; (b) organizing and coordinating; (c) information handling; (d) providing for growth and development; (e) motivating; and (f) conflict handling and strategic problem solving. Managers can vary in the performance of one or more roles at the same time and in different situations.

The Goal Approach

Differences in managerial effectiveness have been used to analyze the goal-setting ability of managers (Locke, 1968). Challenging goals set for oneself and the unit are found to result in a higher level of performance than easy goals, and specific challenging goals result in a higher level of performance than no goals or a generalized goal of 'do' your best. Important attributes of task-work goals, as identified by Locke, are challenge, clarity, involvement, feedback, commitment, acceptance and psychological success. Managers may vary in their ability to communicate the goals to different sub-units and juniors. Orpen (1978) has studied the relationship between the communication of goals and the perceived clarity of the knowledge of these at four levels of employees (director, manager, supervisor and worker) in eight firms. He has reported that the quality and frequency of interactions with the manager determines the clarity of an employee's knowledge of the organization's goals. Managers are thus seen as disseminators of information about organizational goals as they function at different levels.

Managers as decisionmakers are constantly faced with, what Mason and Mitroff (1981) have called, 'Wicked Problems' in the organizations. Some of these are related to the ambiguity of goals and some to the changes and adjustments made in goals. Some problems tend to become more complicated whenever an effort is made to solve them, as the goals also repeatedly change. Effective managers are required to demonstrate their capability to attend to different goals in a well-coordinated manner, and to draw upon the strengths of different viewpoints. They are required to be receptive to new information, to constantly research and experiment with ways to redefine a goal and to identify the associated problems (Schon, 1983). Managers as individuals need a high degree of insight and self-awareness because their own ends and means are continually being reviewed, compromised and changed in interaction with the organizational goals and processes.

The Developmental Approach

In recent years, management theorists have emphasized the need for using the developmental approach to understand and analyze managerial behaviour. The adherents of the structural developmental theory argue that people act on the basis of the meanings that things have for them, meanings that are shaped by the person's attitudes, assumptions, values and beliefs and are collectively called a person's world-view. Individuals' world-views are shaped over the years. These are complex and stable, but can vary for different individuals within the same setting as well as across different settings. The structural theorists (Chomski, 1957; Levi-Strauss, 1963) have made use of the deep universal structures within the human organism to explain the similarity in the world-views of people, in spite of their cultural and other variations.

Some of the structural developmental theories of interpersonal development (Selman, 1980), moral development (Kohlberg, 1969), age development (Loevinger, 1976) and meaning-making (Kegan, 1982) have identified four discrete stages of human development:

Table 1.1: Stages of Human Development

Developmental Theory	Opportunistic stage	Special stage	Goal-oriented stage	Self-defining stage
Kohlberg (1969)	Instrumental orientation	Interpersonal concordance orientation	Societal orientation	Principled orientation
Loevinger (1976)	Opportunistic	Conformist	Conscientious	Autonomus
Selman (1980)	Unilateral authoritarian relations	Fairweather	Stability, Mutual conflict resolution	Interdependence
Kegan (1982)	Imperial	Interpersonal	Institutional	Interindividual

Source: Fisher, Merron and Torbert (1987)

An important feature of the developmental theories has been the consensus on the natural ordering or progression of world-views in a predictable sequence. The four key propositions of the structural developmental theory are:

1. The order of development implies an invariant hierarchical sequence, in which each more evolved world-view represents a more adequate understanding of the world than the prior world-views (Kohlberg, 1969).
2. Individuals holding more evolved world-views develop greater

cognitive abilities and conceptual complexity than those having earlier world-views (Loevinger, 1976).

3. As one matures, one is increasingly able to (a) accept responsibility for the consequences of one's actions; (b) empathize with others who hold a conflicting or dissimilar world-view; and (c) tolerate higher levels of stress and ambiguity (Bartunek, Gordon and Weathersby, 1983).

4. The person holding a more evolved world-view is more attuned to his or her own inner feelings and to the outer environment than the person holding an earlier world-view (Loevinger, 1976).

In the corporate context, the developmental approach implies that the world-views of managers influence the ways in which they structure their conceptions of power, their behaviour appropriateness in different work situations, their task definitions, conflict resolutions, experiences and perceptions and their basic functions of deciding and leading. Indeed, managers by virtue of their position are expected to have highly mature and advanced developmental world-views (Bass, 1985). In order to manage effectively, a manager ought to first occupy the coordination and collaboration stages and then a later stage of development. Managers must undergo developmental changes over the years to be able to remain effective in an organization transforming from one stage to another. Efforts may be made to foster adult development and thereby enhance managerial effectiveness (Fisher, Merron and Torbert, 1987).

The Professional Approach

Researchers using the professional approach to managers' behaviour envisage that work, effort or energy are induced in managers as a result of the flow of role requirements from a profession, and its norm-transmitting associations (Gouldner, 1957). The definitions proposed by Etzioni (1964), Satow (1975), and Vollmer and Mills (1966), and the research on professionals (Hall, 1967; Harrison, 1974; Sorenson and Sorenson, 1974) have led to the development of the following five role prescriptions that combine with appropriate motivational patterns within an individual and induce the work energy necessary for corporate functioning:

1. **Acquiring Knowledge**: The manager as a professional should have a sustained interest in his work and a desire to learn, acquire, transmit and use his/her knowledge and skills.
2. **Independent Action**: The manager should be responsible for his/her actions. He/she must learn to make independent decisions based on his/her professional judgment.
3. **Acceptance of Status**: This involves a particular kind of visibility for the manager that not only attracts attention, but also invites recognition and respect of juniors and users of the service.
4. **Providing Help**: The relationship of the employer and the manager is that of client–professional. A manager as a professional has an obligation to help the client to the extent that it is in the best public interest. This role prescription is comparable to the 'helping power' construct of McClelland (1975).
5. **Professional Commitment**: A strong tie to the management profession requires its members to be responsive to the ethical norms. This tie is mediated and strengthened through a sense of value-based personal identification or commitment.

The Hierarchical Approach

This approach has been used by managers of large bureaucracies, where written formal communications are adopted as a rule. It specifies six roles for managers:

1. **Accepting Authority Figures**: A positive attitude towards seniors is essential to make and keep the function of hierarchical communication operative.
2. **Competitive Activities**: In a hierarchical organization, rewards at the higher levels are relatively scarce and differentially distributed. Managers thus compete with peers to attain rewards, and adopt strategies that would be rewarding.
3. **Assertive Role**: A manager's role requires a 'take charge' attitude. What is needed is a strong desire to be assertive, to be able to demonstrate one's ability to push people to work and to get the job done.
4. **Imposing Wishes**: The position of managers in the hierarchical structure equips them with the powers of manipulation of sanctions and downward supervision. At times it may not

be possible to convince others, and yet managers have to impose their judgment on them.

5. **Standing Out from the Group**: Managers assume visible positions that are clearly differentiated from the relative homogeneity of their subordinates. They deal with people who are junior to them in terms of skill, position, responsibility etc. Their roles require them to act differently.

6. **Functions of Routine Administration**: Routine administrative duties are to be performed by managers in a responsible manner, so that the organization functions smoothly.

The Integrative Approach

The integrative approach to effectiveness has been proposed because effective managers are expected to score high on several dimensions simultaneously. These are: a feeling of being in control of the situation, professional commitment, integration, concern for the performance of others, sensitivity to the rights of co-workers, an openness to changes in the traditional structure of power distribution, and an awareness of profitability, investment returns, efficiency and so on.

A comparative study of the different approaches indicates that effective managers should project the image of individuals who use logical, incremental and dialectical approaches in making decisions (Mason and Mitroff, 1981; Quinn, 1980); are able to balance concerns for people (Blake and Mouton, 1964); are able to vary their behaviour to adopt to a wide variety of situations (Hersey and Blanchard, 1982); and are able to act collaboratively in management action (Merron, Fisher and Torbert, 1987). They should also recognize the role of personal attributes of effort (Porter and Lawler, 1968), the need for achievement and power (McClelland, 1961) and the need for competition (Miner, 1978), as emphasized in some of the earlier motivational theories.

Effective Managers

The successful managers in most corporations have been distinguished from the unsuccessful ones on the basis of interpersonal and other skills. Singh, Kaul and Ahluwalia (1983) have reported that integrative factors, such as leadership, team-spirit and employee's identification with organizational goals, together with innovation and career advancement, contribute to the individual as well as organizational effectiveness of managers. Dayal (1984) has identified the following important factors of effective management:

1. A clear understanding of the mission by the management.
2. Organizational values shared by the management and the employees and related to national goals.
3. Concern for customers and an understanding of what the organization has to do to serve them better.
4. Concern for developing the capabilities of employees at all levels.

Researchers have confirmed that managers as individuals differ in their approach, strategy and effectiveness and will continue to differ despite organizational engineering. It is true that many managers find it futile to try to stimulate excellent performance on the part of others. Some manage 'heroically' by relying on their own technical or administrative skills, others 'transactionally' by enabling followers to fulfil their goals (Bass, 1985; Bradford and Cohen, 1984).

A somewhat different but culture-specific concept of managerial effectiveness—'corporate soul'—has been introduced in the context of Indian organizations by Singh and Paul (1985). They have argued that it gives life and purpose to the organization. Effective organizations exhibit the following four indicators with corresponding processes. These constitute the core of the 'corporate soul':

Table 1.2: The 'Corporate Soul'

Indicators	Processes
1. Integration (High morale, job satisfaction and few grievances of employees)	1. Affection (Human relations, welfare, personnel policies and human development)
2. Actuation (Productivity and surplus)	2. Realization (Sensing changes in environment, planning and innovation)
3. Projection (Reputation and public image, customer satisfaction)	3. Initiation (Personality of the leader, participative culture, enterprise/innovation)
4. Sustenance (Low turnover of employees, sense of belonging, low absenteeism)	4. Restraint (Self-restraint, control and discipline)

Source: Singh and Paul (1985)

Singh and Paul (1985) have used the four-factor model in a number of researches in public, private and professional organizations. They have concluded that in organizational life MOCSHA (Mission, Objectives, Clear Targets, Strategies, Humanization and Activities) provides the complete sequence of linking individual and group actions with organizational objectives and goals. They have drawn up the following modal profile of an effective manager:

1. He/She integrates with other people, rather than keeping a distance from them.
2. He/She builds up teamwork and an image of the organization by contributing to the awareness of the mission of the organization, and creates full job satisfaction.
3. He/She brings in actuation by inculcating a sense of productivity and activism in the organization.
4. He/She projects the right image of the reputation of the organization to the clients and the public.
5. He/She creates a sense of continuity of the organization by creating a positive time perspective and by retaining competent people on the job.
6. He/She feels for the people and the concern for them leads to full control of human relations.
7. He/She scans the environment and realizes the changes.
8. He/She responds to the changes by creative planning and innovation.
9. He/She is the initiator and leads people through his/her dynamism and enterprise.
10. He/She develops a sense of self-restraint amongst the people.

In another study, Sachdev, Pande and Easwaram (1986) have reported that authority, values held by managers, leadership, role clarity, quality of communication in the organization and many other factors are important for managers to perform effectively. Tsui and Ohlott (1988) have found the concepts of ability, motivation and contextual factors as non-role and role behaviour variables useful. Penley, Alexander, Jernigan and Henwood (1991) have observed a relationship between the performance of managers and their communication skills. It seems that, if the organizations can clearly define their purpose and mission, if they can inculcate the desired value system in their employees, if they can build a climate conducive to making people feel responsible, and if they can back up their members and encourage them to take risks and share power, and thereby motivate them towards excellence, they could achieve effectiveness both at the individual and the corporate level. Mintzberg (1991) has recommended that the best way to manage organizations effectively is for managers to focus on building structures, either by using established forms or by combining them. Managing an organization is like building with LEGO blocks—the best structure is the one that balances the forces most gracefully. Just to be sure that things work out well, managers should see that ideology and politics are balanced in their own dynamic equilibrium.

Summary and Direction

To sum up, the conceptualization of effectiveness should include individual as well as organizational attributes, as the dimensions of individual and organizational differences are structurally linked and functionally interdependent. Both emphasize the achievement of goals via efficient operations, satisfaction of needs, and expectations of different levels of constituents. Again, both emphasize multi-level assessments. The organizational dimension focuses on excellence in institutions and systems to which individuals contribute separately and collectively. The individual dimension is individualistic in nature, but it is integral to the group and organizational functioning. There is an urgent need to develop reliable performance indicators to improve managerial competence and thereby help in the better management of public and private sector corporations (Carter, 1991).

Irrespective of the theoretical model used, all organizations are expected to be structurally sound and functional, and managers as individuals in all organizations are expected to be efficient and successful in achieving the set targets. Their success and effectiveness should be contingent on dynamic interactions among a multitude of factors like their loci in the socio-organizational system (particularly social, politico-economic controls and organizational systems), their own socio-psychological characteristics and their systems of functioning.

Corporations as well as individuals are embedded in the given social systems which shape and affect their culture, ethos, values, roles, expectations and dispositions in an ongoing manner. In fact, social systems retain the final sanctioning authority, and thus regulate the limits of stability/change in the corporate system and in individuals. The extent of their success will be mirrored through the effectiveness of organizations and managers as individuals. In any corporate set-up, how the managers utilize their position and resources to function effectively, to relate to each other, to exercise power, to act in harmony with national and social objectives, and to further the interests of the organization and the employees, will define their level of success/effectiveness. This is an appropriate theme at this stage and worth investigating from the point of view of theory as well as that of practice.

2

ISSUES IN CORPORATE MANAGEMENT AND THE PROBE

Identification of the Problem

The experiences, perspectives and perceptions of researchers and practitioners often underlie the choice of issues considered relevant for debate/ investigation. These frequently tend to vary; more so in terms of the priorities assigned as these are relative judgments. It may thus be considered appropriate to derive the logic of choice from more than one source of information in the identification of the issues of corporate management: (*a*) The logic underlying the objectives and structures of the corporate set-up in the country; (*b*) the available theoretical evidence; and (*c*) a first-hand preliminary probe.

Corporate Complexity

The modern corporate system is complex in nature and faces multiple challenges in the environment, both national and international. Corporations vary according to the type of control, provisions, products, networking of interpersonal relations, and demands made on their managers. Specifically in India, the variety of policy and resource constraints, laws, the regulatory apparatus, the developmental objectives of the public sector, the nature of control and ownership in the private sector, and the restrictive role of financial institutions and holding companies make the corporate operations much more complex and the managers' position in the corporate system quite unique and critical.

Corporate Set-up in India

In post-Independence India, planners and politicians have adopted a model of mixed economy in which public and private sectors coexist, more as a historic necessity than as a choice. The roles of public and private enterprises are embodied in the first Industrial Policy Statement of the Government of India (1948), and subsequently reiterated in the Industrial Policy Resolutions of 1956 and 1980 of the Government of India. It has been recognized that the adoption of the socialistic pattern of society as a national objective and the need for planned and rapid development necessitate that all industries of basic and strategic importance, requiring large investments or being in the nature of public utility services, should be in the public sector. Thus, the basic and infrastructural industries having long gestation periods and low profitability were kept in the public sector, while the profit-making and consumer-oriented industries were included in the private sector. In the public sector, the government has full ownership rights and responsibilities under the Bureau of Public Enterprises. In the private sector, the major ownership rights remain in the hands of private individuals and groups, with some government nominees and representatives of financial institutions on their Boards.

The public sector has been advocated in India for three reasons: (*a*) to gain control of the commanding heights of the economy; (*b*) to promote critical development in terms of social gains or strategic value rather than primarily considerations of profit; and (*c*) to provide commercial surpluses with which to finance further economic development.

Over the years, both the public sector and the private sector have expanded. The public sector popularly symbolizes the progressive or the socialist approach which is against the private sector expanding by following a capitalist and profit-oriented approach. The overall objectives of the public sector have significantly influenced the industrial policy in general, and specifically the policy governing the administration or control of prices, the location of public enterprises, labour legislation, manpower planning, and import and investment decisions. The 'objective-parameters' adopted for the functioning of the public sector have been viewed as goals to be achieved via implementation of the successive Five-Year Plans, making the state the principal instrument of economic and social transformation, and the determiner of all development strategies (D'Souza, 1984; Khandwalla, 1984). The functioning of the private sector is determined much more freely by the owners in the given market conditions.

Achievements

The public sector in India is extensive and intimately tied up with planned development and government investment. It has grown to the extent that central public enterprises have an investment of over Rs. 610 billion and they employ 2.2 million people (which is approximately 50 per cent of the gross investment in the economy and 70 per cent of total employment in the organized sector). Apart from the central government, state and local governments have established public sector enterprises or taken over production from other kinds of units. Qualitatively, public sector corporations have achieved higher standards of conditions of work, employee welfare and remunerations. Remote and backward areas of the country have been the beneficiary of various infrastructural facilities, social amenities and overall development. Research and development facilities have been set up in the basic industries which have helped in the development of highly-skilled manpower (general and specialist). The private sector has also grown in size. It has improved in quality of management, technology, and diverse product types, and has in many ways benefited from developments in the public sector.

Problems

The objectives of the public sector have increased over the years. Each of the multiple objectives accrues to the units extra costs and additional managerial responsibility, but only limited scope for price adjustments and thus, small profits. The tight control of the public sector enterprises by various government agencies has eroded their autonomy, accountability and role performance. Public sector enterprises have less autonomy, more bosses, more objectives, more diffused public accountability and more political interference than their private sector counterparts (Brown, 1984; Dutt, 1981; Krishnaswamy, 1980; Singh and Pant, 1982). The issues of technological upgradation, higher productivity targets, cost and quality consciousness and customer service have been recurrently pushed to the backyard. The need for organizational innovations in the prevailing industrial environment has not been recognized. The people's expectations of results from public enterprises have also not been realized. The deepening resource crunch has brought to the forefront the need to adopt measures of cost-effective production and development. The liberalization of policies has been linked to efficiency improvement, bringing into focus the need to develop effective managers, systems and procedures.

The balance-sheet at the end of nearly four decades indicates that the public sector has singularly failed to deliver. Collectively, the 244 central public sector undertakings, if the petroleum sector is excluded, do not yield more than one per cent return on investments. The records happen to be even more dismal for state government enterprises. It has been reported by the Ministry of Programme Implementation (MPI) that many of the public sector projects suffer from time and cost overruns. The foremost delaying factor has been the transfer of project coordinators at the top. A survey of projects each costing more than Rs. 50 crores has shown a comparatively short tenure of the top functionaries and a vapour-thin response of the government to the phenomenon. Delays have been attributed to many factors: the difficulties at the 'pre-investment and project preparation stage'; the clearance from the Forest and Environment Ministry and other clearances from concerned regulatory agencies; inadequate planning for infrastructural development; the requirement of obtaining equipment from indigenous supplies and the consequent delay in the supply of critical equipment; non-sequential supply and mismatch of equipment; organizational weaknesses in the project management including the non-availability of managerial talent of a high order; and the span of managerial charge and mid-stream changes in the nature and scope of the projects. This does not, however, absolve the managers of their responsibilities.

In fact, in the 1980 Industrial Policy document, it has been explicitly stated that effective operational systems of management should be evolved in public sector undertakings. The public sector needs to be identified as a people's sector and not as 'nobody's sector'.

Management in the public sector should regard and appreciate the fact that the public sector is for the public and of the public who virtually own it. They are 'professional managers' and thus a category of employees distinct from the owners.

As the public sector has been unable to cope with the challenge of becoming competitive and resource generating, the executives and managers have recently been criticized by the public and politicians alike for macroeconomic policy failures. Although the problems arise from multiple sources and in a complex manner, the public sector continues to treat them as unilinear. It has been observed that the efforts to improve the effectiveness of public sector enterprises need 'perestroika' in economic policies as well as in organizational structuring and managerial practices. Different public sector corporations have different problems and challenges and demand different solutions. No uniform policy can be prescribed for all corporations/organizations. Each unit is unique and demands the use of different approaches and managerial styles that depend on size, nature, employee attitudes and beliefs, and planned targets.

In view of the recent increasing pressures towards greater privatization and competitiveness in the context of the opening up of the national economy and the increasing globalization at the international level, there is an urgent need to evolve new management systems to make organizations responsive to changing economic, social and political environments. There is need to integrate the developmental needs of the country with the aspirations of the people and the requirements of the public and private sectors, as strategically both together have the potential to contribute vital inputs to the socioeconomic development of the people.

The five key constraints on public sector managers, which have been listed by Ring and Perry (1985), seem relevant to the public sector in India. These may be stated in terms of the following five propositions:

1. **Policy Ambiguity**: Policy directives tend to be more ill-defined for the public sector than for the private sector. The policy is not very clear and does not facilitate the functioning of the private sector either.
2. **The Openness of the Government**: The relative openness of the decision-making process creates greater constraints for public sector executives and managers than for their private

sector counterparts. Private sector managers have greater freedom of making strategic choices and implementing them.

3. **The Attentive Public**: Public sector policymakers are generally subject to more direct and sustained influence from a greater number of political and other interest groups than are managers in the private sector. The private sector is not necessarily obliged to accept the influence/ advice of any particular group, if their interests clash.

4. **The Time Problem**: Public sector managers have to cope with time constraints that are more artificial and externally determined than those that confront private sector managers. The private sector can set its own framework of time.

5. **Shaky Coalitions**: The policy legitimation coalitions are by nature less stable in the public sector and are more prone to disintegrate during policy implementation under different political bosses. The coalitions in the private sector are often of family members and more stable.

Evidence

The structural problems inherent in the setting up of public sector organizations lead to delays, disjointed authority and lack of responsibility (Dayal 1973). The public sector corporations have been placed under the concerned ministries, but the bureaucracy in India has failed to cope with new administrative goals because of its highly structured roles, pattern of interactions and value orientations. The public sector organizations have not been judged effective because of (a) political interference, and (b) red tapism (Sinha, 1973). The rigid hierarchy of structures has resulted in distorted communication (Agarwal, 1974).

The initiation of any structural changes in the public sector would require primarily changes in employee attitudes. The adopted structures should motivate people to a qualitatively higher level of thinking and working and dissuade them from conforming to routine. Each corporation should perceive the challenges for itself and aspire for different levels of achievement, by using different strategies and tactics. For example, what worked in Bharat Heavy Electricals Ltd. (BHEL) is the introduction of a planning structure, stress on research and development (R & D), continuous technological upgradation followed by improvements in the quality of products and services; in Maruti Udyog Ltd., it is the work culture and the work environment; and in the case of the Steel Authority of India Ltd. (SAIL), it is the system of signing a Memorandum of Understanding (MoU) with the Government of India, apart from the exercise of communicating the possible solutions to problems.

The public sector remains highly dependent on the government and government-controlled organizations for resources and thus makes greater use of the boundary-spanning mechanisms directed at the government. The interactions among mixed economy, scarcities, political democracy and tight state control have promoted a parallel economy in the country in which the efficiency-oriented managerial rationality has been substituted by a corruption-oriented rationality (Bidani and Mitra, 1982). This has weakened the position of the public sector and increasingly marginalized the role of competent and professional managers.

The strategic management of the public sector entails management of uncertainties, rigidities, complexities and discontinuities, as compared with the uncertainties, flexibilities and not so many discontinuities in the private sector. This requires that managers have access to updated information about their jurisdiction and the political climate, the ability to define the management task clearly, a high level of technical expertise, adaptability and negotiability, and the ability to establish and exercise their authority. Some challenges for managers in the two sectors arise from significant differences between the organizational climates of public and private sectors (Roy, 1974; Sinha, 1973), managers' values and motivations (Kakar, 1972), and leadership styles (Sinha, 1980). Molnar and Rogers (1976) have defined the effectiveness of public agencies in terms of either their ability to distribute resources or to provide services to the environment and not in terms of profits, which may be the case in the private sector. Mohr (1983) has warned that managers in the public as well as in the private sector would have to walk the tight rope between goal clarity and orientation towards maximizing profits, as the pursuit of one does not necessarily lead to the achievement of the other.

A large number of chief executives of public sector units have a technical background, more so than those of private sector units, and yet their performance does not demonstrate any advantage accruing from it (Satyanand, 1984). On an average, public sector managers rank profitability much lower than what private sector managers do. Good industrial relations are ranked significantly higher by the former, but coping with environmental changes is seen as much more important by the latter (FORE, 1984). In the private sector, family feuds and extensive generational conflicts operate negatively (Agarwal, 1984), while in the public sector there are inevitable conflicts with the bureaucracy and the ministry concerned. The available evidence in fact tends to reinforce an image of inward, production and function-related management of the public sector against the outward, adaptive and profitability-oriented management of the private sector.

Preliminary Probe

If one has to believe what one sees then one has no substitute but to gather first-hand information in order to evolve unambiguous, workable and realistic procedures for understanding the underlying constraints and challenges faced by senior and top-level managers of public and private sector enterprises. One also has to identify the crucial variables which may make a difference in the effective performance of enterprises and their managers. Preliminary discussions were thus held with chairmen/managing directors of some public enterprises as a first step. The situation of the corporate sector in the country and the objectives of the investigation were kept in focus. Out of the entire list of public sector corporations and central government undertakings prepared by the Bureau of Public Enterprises, 35 corporations of diverse types (based on size, product, status) were identified and the chairmen/managing directors were approached for an early meeting.

A total number of 18 chairmen/managing directors responded favourably and agreed to meet me. These executives belonged to enterprises oriented to assembly-line production, power generation, chemicals and fertilizers, trading and services. The discussions were open, broad-based, general and policy-oriented, although they focused on enterprise-specific problems. This provided a tremendous insight into the problems of managers, their experiences and perceptions of the tasks, challenges at hand and future prospects. Some new dimensions were added to the envisaged plan. A summary of the crucial points that emerged from these discussions is presented below:

1. Although public sector enterprises vary in orientation, size, products and specified tasks and are labeled autonomous, not much of the autonomy is experienced by managers in reality. There is a uniformly high degree of dependence on the government. The prevalent structural and functional arrangements have made the managers dependent on the government and the bureaucracy in their day-to-day functioning. Even the top executives have not been able to make any substantial decisions without the concurrence of the concerned ministry. This has eroded their image and authority vis-à-vis internal and external functioning. The situation happens to be somewhat more difficult in the case of enterprises which are either not generating high profits or have been incurring recurrent losses. ·

2. Political considerations continue to weigh heavily in the process of corporate decision-making. As a rule, rather than the exception, the concerned ministries treat the corporations as their extended jurisdictions. Decisions are often made in an ad hoc manner, extended, reversed and modified, depending on the will of the political bosses. This style of functioning reflects negatively on the professional commitment of managers who, if allowed to use their professionalism in a positive manner, may be able to turn around the public sector into an instrument of growth. The unproductive work culture of ministries has been deliberately transplanted to the corporations, and this has debased the professionalism of managers who have high technical and managerial qualifications, but make no use of them.

3. The topman is unanimously considered important. He is known to set the tone of the corporation. His selection thus ought to be made as judiciously and objectively as possible. He should be allowed to function without any interference in the interests of the corporation.

4. The targeted corporate goals are deliberately kept ambiguous, unrealistic, flexible, negotiable and changed under internal and external pressures. The unit heads are not clear about their targets, nor are they able to communicate these clearly to their juniors. Also there are hardly any links perceived between the goals set and the roles assigned.

5. While time management constitutes an important component of the management of any modern corporate body, it has been given nominal importance in the public sector. Even on time-

limit projects, decisions are deliberately delayed and made only under pressure, and resources are curtailed and shifted around in an ad hoc manner, thereby undermining the fact that this only adds to the corporate losses. No one has subsequent feelings of guilt. More time is happily spent by managers on meeting their superiors just to satisfy their inflated egos rather than on work activities. Long meetings are constantly held at different levels, at times with an agenda, at times without it, but the outcomes are trivial, routine and lacking in direction.

6. Senior managers prefer not to be involved in proactive, sound, forward-looking strategy-making behaviour. They do everything possible to discourage innovations in the corporate sector, as this might invite the anger of the political bosses above and the people below. The taking of risks, if necessary, is kept to a bare minimum as there is no appreciation for such action. A 'wait and watch' approach is found to be more rewarding than making quick decisions and implementing them through appropriate action. The lengthy and cumbersome procedures of functioning which have evolved in corporations on the model of ministries do not suit corporate goals. These invariably lead to cost overruns, and consequent inefficiencies and a deflated employee morale. An alternative model of operation is needed, but attempts have not been made to find it in principle.

7. The environment of business has changed over the years. It has become quite dynamic and uncertain, needing a preparedness on the part of managers to cope with diverse and heterogeneous pressures. Yet changes/adjustments in structures of corporations have not occurred. These are not welcomed and considered to be difficult as well as trouble making. All decisions relating to the expansion and diversification of products, that should have been made at the corporate level, are finalized in the concerned ministries, keeping in view the numerous political and other considerations rather than the capacity of the corporation. On many occasions, the decisions taken are not liked by the employees. The information flow within the corporation is restricted and inadequate. Managers have to manage, without having a reward power to control or motivate the marginal employees. Senior managers face pressures, both from above and from below, and feel quite helpless in the prevalent situation.

8. The political parties have patronized the unions and labour legislation has proved to be lop-sided. The process of disciplinary action has been made so tough and unrealistic by labour legislation and unions that no one really wants to be involved in it. Productivity is neither valued at any level nor demanded. Employees have nothing at stake, even if the corporations are in the red. Industries like power and petroleum have been able to generate some profits only because of the protected and monopolistic policies of the government, and not because of their competitive position or managerial competence.

9. The socio-political objectives prescribed for the public sector are too many and too costly; they are eating into its vitals and consuming its profits. The capacity utilization of most corporations has remained low because of bad planning and unionization at all levels.

10. Successful corporations that function well are few in number and relatively more open. They encourage participative decision-making and involvement, unlike loss-making or marginally operating corporations. In the former, human relations are relatively better, innovations are definitely appreciated, planning is regarded as an essential function, and some visible links are demonstrated between goals and activities. Further, personnel development programmes are taken much more seriously by management and employees.

11. It is felt that the policy of reservations (as laid down in the Constitution) should only be applied at the stage of initial recruitment and not to the question of promotion. Competence should not be compromised once the entry is made. Institution building should be given more attention as a long-term policy. This requires sound policies, greater resource mobilization, higher levels of competence among employees and sound management.

Propositions

A critical appraisal of the objectives and complexity of the corporate set-up, the available evidence and the response analysis of the preliminary discussions suggest that any meaningful probe must adopt a multi-method and multi-variate framework to assess managerial performance. Managerial effectiveness is a multidimensional outcome of numerous variables (personal, social and organizational), and should be assessed by using multiple criteria like goal achievement, role perceptions, confidence and professional commitment of managers. Secondly, it may not be possible or desirable to obtain all the data by using standardized scales. The qualitative methods should be given adequate weight in the corporate enquiry. Further, the crucial issue of senior managers having a heightened ego problem should not be allowed to contaminate the data-gathering process. This has been contained by an a priori decision of the project director to collect data personally with the support of research investigators.

It seems plausible to assume that the effectiveness of managers in public and private sectors may follow different paths. The focus of the problem should be on examining the operation of personal, social and organizational determinants of managerial effectiveness in the public sector vis-à-vis the private sector.

The specific propositions may be stated as follows:

1. The Sectoral identities, profit status of corporations and personal orientations of managers make a difference in time management, choice of strategy, perceptions of environment, structure, goal achievement, role perceptions, confidence and professional commitment.

2. Sectoral identities and profit status of corporations matter in the personal orientations of managers.

3. Personal orientations of managers are differentially related to choice of strategy, perceptions of environment and structure in different corporate sectors and in corporations having different profit status.

4. The aspects of time management relate differentially to manager's strategy-making, perceptions of environment, structure, goal achievement, role perceptions, confidence and professional commitment.

5. The variables of time management, strategy-making, perceptions of environment and structure differentially contribute to variance in goal achievement, role perceptions, confidence and professional commitment of managers.

Conceptual Model

The conceptual model to be used is given below:

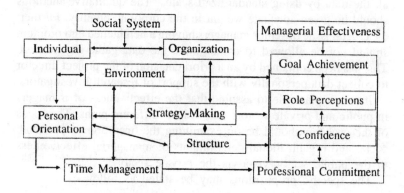

Social System

All individuals and organizations are situated within a broader social system that constrains the forms these can assume and the manner in which these can function. In the given social reality, issues related to social and cultural milieu, economic development, technology import and development, political and other considerations operate as relevant context factors and affect managerial effectiveness (Chaudhuri, 1980; Dayal, 1967; and Sinha, 1980). The general culture of the society percolates into the organizations, and affects the individual and organizational interpretations of norms and procedures, and institutionalizes the ideas, which in turn support its decisions and structures.

Sample Identification

Corporations and managers constitute the sample and were selected in the following manner:

Corporations

Corporations were identified by keeping in view the diversity of corporate purposes, processes, and products (production, services, petroleum, fertilizers, power, automobiles etc.), capacity utilization, profitability, growth in capital and assets over the last five years. A total number of twenty public sector corporations (profit-and loss-making) and eight private sector enterprises were finally selected.

Managers

In the selected corporations, beginning from the top downwards (excluding chairmen/managing directors), 300 managers at two or three levels (directors, general managers, deputy general managers), depending on the corporate structures, were identified. Each manager was personally contacted by the project director on more than three and less than five occasions. In case a manager did not respond favourably or did not make himself/herself available on the fifth occasion, he/she was left out. Complete data were collected on 268 managers in the public sector and on 46 managers in the private sector.

Expectations

It has been the expectation that this study will bridge some of the gaps in the knowledge and understanding of the dynamics of the effectiveness of managers in different settings. In a recent review, Khandwalla (1988) has noted similar critical issues in corporate management, namely, configuration of context, management goals, style, strategy, structure, systems and processes that make managers and organizations effective/ineffective. These need attention. An investigation into these issues should throw sufficient light on the attitudes prevalent among politicians, planners and the public. These are formed on the mistaken assumption of equal effectiveness or the lack of it among all managers. To enhance the practical and theoretical relevance of the findings, the conceptualization of the problem, the approach and the analysis have been made broad-based. They are not limited to a model. Further, this study is unique in its focus on senior managers who control the nerve centres of corporations, are hard-pressed for time and are difficult to be approached by researchers in general.

3

PERSONAL ORIENTATION, STRATEGY-MAKING, ENVIRONMENT AND STRUCTURE

Managerial Contingencies

Most modern organizations recruit managers at different levels of hierarchical set-up and distinguish them in terms of necessary qualifications, experience, responsibilities and perks offered. Recruitment of managers to a particular level frequently includes persons having compatible professional skills and preparation. They are provided equitable treatment. Yet all managers working at the same level do not demonstrate similar perceptions, attitudes and behavioural outcomes. Researchers have investigated the influence of contextual variables on individual and organizational attributes, but the available evidence is inconclusive. It is expected that personal orientations of managers, strategy-making, perceptions of environment and structure will vary in corporations in different sectors and in corporations having different profit status.

Personal Orientation

Concept

Personal orientation is commonly known as the internal- external locus of control. It refers to a person's generalized beliefs about the degree to which he or she can, by his or her own behaviour, control the reinforcement and outcomes in life. Internal–external construct has been viewed by Rotter (1966) as a generalized expectancy, which operates over a variety of situations and affects the individual's functioning. While there are situations in which a person would find it possible or impossible to have control on one's outcomes, in reality one encounters a variety of situations in which the probability of personal control is often indeterminable. In these situations the externality-oriented individuals (externals) tend to doubt characteristically the potential of their behaviour in influencing outcomes, while the internality-oriented individuals (internals) tend to believe that their behaviour can affect such outcomes.

Personal orientation has been related to numerous forms of organizational behaviour at the individual and collective levels (Kogan and Wallach, 1964). Some researchers indicate that externals tend to feel more alienated from their work-place than internals (Mitchell, 1975; Seeman, 1967; and Wolfe, 1972). Externals as leaders tend to use coercive power, while internals rely more on persuasive forms of power (Goodstadt and Hjelle, 1973). Internals are more considerate supervisors (Pryer and Distefano, 1971) and experience greater enjoyment in a participative work environment (Mitchell, Smyser and Weed, 1975). Internals are more activity-oriented and more likely than externals to possess entrepreneurial qualities (Shapero, 1975). Internals are also more satisfied with their work than externals are (Organ and Greene, 1974).

Phares (1976) has observed that in contrast to externals, internals tend to exert greater effort in controlling their environment, exhibit better learning, seek new information more actively when that information has personal relevance, use information better, and are more concerned with information than with the social demands of situations. Internals respond to reinforcement contingencies on the job and demonstrate initiative and personal action. Internals as managers are more task-oriented and function better in stress situations than externals (Anderson, 1977). Internals as chief executives pursue product–market innovation, undertake greater risks, and lead the competitors (Miller, Kets de Vries and Toulouse, 1982). Externals are unresponsive to incentives and prefer direct supervision (Spector, 1982).

Measure

The manager's personal orientation has been measured by using Rotter's internal–external scale. The scale measures an individual's perception of how much control he/she is able to exert over the events in life. An internality-oriented person should feel confident that the outcomes of his/her behaviour are the consequent of his/her own efforts. An externality-oriented person, on the other hand tends to believe that the events in his/her life are beyond his/her control and can be attributed to fate, luck or destiny etc.

The scale consists of 29 pairs of statements of which six are feeler items. The respondent is required to read one pair of statements at a time and then respond to the statement that could be true about himself/herself. If some respondents believe that either both the items are true or none are true they are asked to select a statement which is more nearly true than not true in their position. They are also told not to be influenced by their previous choice when responding to subsequent statements. The statements are scored in the direction of externality, in that one point has been given for each 'external' response to a question. The higher the score on the scale, the more external would be the person.

Strategy-Making

Either as individuals or in groups, most managers make decisions to tackle an array of situational and psychological pressures in their functioning. They make decisions sometimes on the basis of objective information and rationality and sometimes on the basis of their cognition of the world (Anderson and Paine, 1975; Das, 1986; Mitchell, Rediker and Beach, 1986). In the process of decision-making they use strategies that take into account individual and organizational attributes, although they place more emphasis on the latter. Strategies are not considered akin to organizational goals and styles of top management. Cameron (1986b) has considered managerial strategies to be more important than structures, demographics, finance etc.

A strategy represents a composite pattern in the sequence of actions. Many researchers have preferred to utilize a decision-making perspective to understand the various processes involved in strategy-making. Lewin (1951) has observed that like all human behaviour, strategic decisions are influenced by forces and events in the past, the present and those anticipated in the future, as all the forces and events combine to create the psychological context for each decision. The choice of a particular strategy in an organization results from a stream of decisions and reflects an aggregate pattern of behaviours that occur over time (Fredrickson, 1983, 1984, 1985, 1986). Quinn (1980) and Bourgeois (1980) have treated strategy formulation as a decision-making process.

It has been assumed that managerial strategies can vary along a number of dimensions, such as competitiveness, innovation, risk-taking, proactivity and futurity and so on. Differences in choice of strategy may also be related to the temporal orientations of organizations. A strong past or present orientation may lead to a defender-type strategy, whereas a strong future orientation may be associated with a prospector-type strategy (Miles and Snow, 1978).

Managers using proactive strategies and strategies with an external emphasis have been found more successful than those using internal and reactive strategies. Multifaceted strategies are more effective than monolithic strategies. Porter (1980) has argued that innovation happens to be one of the key strategies with which businessmen attempt to differentiate themselves from competitors. The important managerial attitudes and behaviours in organizations pursuing innovation as a strategy are expertise, acceptance of challenge, and a long-term focus. The use of such a strategy requires experimentation, which makes frequent failures probable and real.

A few Indian researchers have investigated the effects of growth and turnaround strategies on organizational functioning (Balakrishnan, Bhargava and Jain, 1980; Bidani and Mitra, 1982; Chakraborty and Dixit, 1992; Chaudhuri and Khandwalla, 1983; Chaudhuri, Kumar, Prahlad and Vathsala, 1982; George, 1984; Khandwalla, 1981; Maheshwari and Malhotra, 1977; Padaki, 1984; and Prahlad and Thomas, 1977). Little work has been done on proactivity, innovation and other strategies. In Indian studies, the focus of innovation has been on product development rather than on its use as a strategy (Chaganti, 1979). Chaganti has noted that in the developmental milieu of India, the higher the echelon of the government, the higher should be the innovation proneness of the agent. Khandwalla (1984) has identified a number of contextual factors that influence positively the innovation-orientation of an organization's management.

Strategy has been considered here as a pattern in the stream of actions. Four types of strategies—innovation, risk-taking, proactivity and futurity—are included.

Innovation

Innovation in organizations can refer to practices/ products that are either global or are specific to an organization. This distinction is necessary to make any innovation in organizations. Innovations can be affected by a diverse array of factors such as a turbulent operating environment, the vulnerability of the organization, client sophistication, variability and diversity of outputs, higher performance targets, a crisis situation, buoyant markets or previous success and the personal attributes of those who make strategic decisions. Innovation as a managerial strategy has been defined here to include the desire to innovate new products, engage in R & D activities, and try out new methods of service or production.

Risk-Taking

Risk-taking implies that failures are quite likely. Not only action, but even inaction involves certain risks. It may be logical for a confident, active and rational manager to take action as and when necessary rather than not act. One would have to accept, however, that some actions involve more risks than others. In the risk-taking strategy, a manager has to take the chance for achieving success, given the overall situation which does not overrule adverse consequences. Although the chances of success and failure are 50:50 in any risk-taking, a manager has to act to transform it into a 100 per cent success. Alternatively, one has to accept that it may entail a 100 per cent failure.

Proactivity

This strategy refers to the individual manager's tendency to be proactive, to lead rather than to follow the competition. Proactive managers take the lead in the choice of products, methods and processes, etc., and function as models for others.

Futurity

Futurity refers to the degree of planning that managers attempt in their organizational roles. All organizations have the planning function, but some may insist on its pursuance, and do so more rigorously than others. Futurity may also relate to a manager's disposition and experience in the organization and to the environmental complexity.

The strategy of innovation is positively related to the complementary strategies of risk-taking, proactivity and futurity (Miller et al., 1982). Risk-taking embraces the probability of failure. Proactive managers put pressure on others to act in a similar direction. Some managers undertake planning as a more natural activity than others. The use of strategies of innovation, risk-taking, proactivity and futurity is related to the personal orientation of managers.

Environment

Turbulence/instability in the environment outside the organization poses a constant threat to its stability. The top executives/managers are required to be highly sensitive to these changes to be able to cope with the stress and strain. These affect the organizations at the aggregate, intermediate and individual levels in a complex manner, defying good definitions and assessments. Burns and Stalker (1961) have found the rate of environmental change to be a determinant of the type of organizational structure that would prove most effective for organizational functioning.

It has been found that one or two 'dominant environmental requirements' may typically dominate any one industry's landscape (Lawrence and Lorsch, 1967). These requirements include technological uncertainty, regulatory demands, raw material shortages, or supply–demand imbalances. Environmental domination of organizations can vary, but these always involve external control over scarce resources and are thus problematic in some way or the other (Pfeffer and Salancik, 1978). Duncan (1972) has operationalized environments on a dynamic–stable and simple–complex continuum. In real life people make use of the cognitive processes in categorizing their environments as certain or uncertain. They show variations in the mapping processes related to their perceived environmental characteristics, cognitive processes, behavioural response repertoire and social expectations (Downey, Hellriegel and Slocum, 1977).

Murdia (1978) has found that in organizations facing the precarious task environment, the decision-making, communications, and coordination structures are more participative, decentralized and organic in type. Hambrick (1981) has identified two sources of critical contingencies for organizations: environment and strategy. He has observed that both can affect internal processes in an ongoing manner. Modern economies operate essentially in environments that are inherently dynamic and complex and the predictors of uncertainty have roots in both personal and environmental domains. How the environmental turbulence will be perceived by the executives and how they will cope with it shall depend on their cognitive–affective attributes (Singhal, 1982).

Environment has been conceptualized as having two dimensions, namely, dynamism and heterogeneity. In corporate environments these two dimensions are known to be reflected in the demand for innovative products, the search for new and different markets, and in the offer of a wide latitude for achievement. Product lines can and should change more often and in many possible ways to cope successfully with the environment.

Structure

Organizations can be structured in many ways (Miles and Snow, 1978). Structure may be described as the formal configuration of roles and procedures, the prescribed framework of the organization, the patterned regularities and interactions, and the processes and alternative modes of departmentalization (Galbraith, 1977; Thompson, 1967). It may also include durable and formal mechanisms that are needed for reducing the uncertainty in decision-making, for facilitating the performance of diverse activities in the organization, and for integrating and coordinating these activities (Khandwalla, 1973). The properties of structure have important consequences for organizational effectiveness. They determine the extent of functional differentiation and the degree of integration, connectedness and 'coupling'. They provide descriptions of how managers (actors) actually transact their work, formulate policy and allocate resources. Ranson, Hinings and Greenwood (1980) have argued that a theoretical framework for the analysis of organizational structures should be underpinned by modes of analysis that are of meaning and causation. Such modes should seek to understand the purposes that actors attach to their conduct and yet preserve the necessity of explaining the complex outcomes of events, whether intentional or not.

Contingency theorists have examined the relationships between organizational structure and environment (Burns and Stalker, 1961; Khandwalla, 1972; Lawrence and Lorsch, 1967; Thompson, 1967), strategy and structure (Chandler, 1962; Rumelt, 1974) and environment and strategy (Miller and Friesen, 1983; Mintzberg, 1973). Researches by Miles and Snow (1978), Mintzberg (1978) and Miller and Friesen (1984) have demonstrated some common configurations among strategic, structural and environmental variables. The researches by Collins and Moore (1970); Kets de Vries and Miller (1984); Miller, Kets de Vries and Toulouse (1982); Miller, Toulouse and Belanger (1985); and Miller and Toulouse (1986) have demonstrated that the particular organizational configurations reflect the personalities of their chief executives. In a subsequent study, Miller and Dröge (1986) have observed that executives' need for achievement and the size of the organization have strong relationships to structural constructs. Technology and uncertainty have little impact on structure.

Indian researchers have so far paid scant attention to problems of structure. Such problems include the different types of structure, the hierarchy of authority and its consequences, and functional and role specialization and their consequences (FORE, 1984; Mishra, 1982; Narain, 1981; Padaki, 1984). Technology has been used in organizations as a dimension of structure (Pugh, Hickson, Hinings and Turner, 1968, 1969) as well as a process for changing inputs into outputs. One of its covariates happens to be the activation of higher order needs in the staff (Khandwalla, 1977). Technology has helped in predicting the differentiation aspect of structural complexity (Singh, 1985). The use of differentiation as an aspect of structure requires managers to be more participative and professional as they have the need to manage multiple cultures prevalent in the organization. Over the years, administrative tasks have become increasingly complex and non-routine due to environmental uncertainty faced by organizations. Executives who have a high 'n-ach' want to have complete control and like to get a feedback from their work environments, and thus embrace more formalized, complex and centralized structures.

Several studies have reported that the control environment in India has far-reaching strategic and structural effects on the Indian public as well as on private sector organizations (Bidani and Mitra, 1982; Brown, 1984; Khandwalla, 1982; Maheshwari and Malhotra, 1977; Murthy, 1982; Patel, 1981). These controls include business house controls and legal/ quasi-legal constraints such as monopolistic trade and restrictive practices on the expansion of private enterprises; regulatory mechanisms on the public sector; and requirements imposed by financial institutions and holding companies. Given the fact that environmental complexity and turbulence are common to enterprises in the public sector and to large private sector enterprises, managers may have some common needs. In India, technology—related growth and turnaround strategies have been considered to be important according to Balakrishnan, Bhargava and Jain (1980); Bidani and Mitra (1982), Chaudhuri (1980) and George (1984).

Three important aspects of structure are scanning, technocratization and differentiation. Scanning has been found useful as a structural variable to make an active search in the environment and to negotiate with various relevant agencies. Technocratization can be used for the identification, manufacture and import of appropriate technology. Differentiation is useful for the development of new lines, sophisticated organizational systems etc.

Scanning

Scanning has been defined as the process of learning about events and trends in the organization's environments. It is a form of 'coping by information' (Hickson, Pugh and Pheysey, 1969). It has been consistently documented as a strikingly informal activity, conducted to some extent by all senior and top-level executives (Aguilar, 1967; Kefalas and Schoderback, 1973; and Hambrick, 1979). Scanning has no rigid structural bounds and appears to be a more fluid base of power. For the purpose of discovering the shifting needs of customers and for developing strategies of competitors, scanning can be particularly useful if the environment is dynamic and the corporation tries to innovate within such an environment. Scanning should also help to ensure that innovations are appropriate (Tushman, 1977).

Technocratization

Organizational technocratization has been used to measure the inclusion and importance of professionals (engineers, technologists, scientists, managers) in the decision-making processes. Innovative corporations are known to be more technocratic because they need expertise in areas of planning, designing and marketing etc. (Hage and Aiken 1967). Particularly in a developing context, the organization's technological capability develops as the organization accumulates experience in task accomplishment. Initially corporations tend to import foreign technology, and then develop their own technological capability by exerting indigenous efforts for the assimilation and improvement of imported foreign technologies.

Differentiation

Innovation adds complexity and diversification to the corporate structure by prompting the use of technocratic departments. But these organizations become highly differentiated to reduce the uncertainty created by environmental dynamism and heterogeneity (Lawrence and Lorsch, 1967). It is believed that effective organizations would attempt a high degree of differentiation together with integration. Differentiation measures the variety among the products and processes used in different corporations.

Strategy, Environment and Structure Scale

A somewhat lengthy questionnaire used by Miller et al. (1982) has been adopted to obtain information on strategy, environment and structure. In the original questionnaire of Miller et al. each question has been formulated in the form of a pair of statements and a seven-point response scale has been used to rate the statements.

In the initial stages when this questionnaire was discussed by the team of two researchers with two senior managers, it appeared that the questionnaire created a false and unfavourable impression. It was felt that a person was expected to read too many statements and then rate them. Most senior managers said that they were hard-pressed for time, and it was feared that the mere idea of completing such a questionnaire would prompt them to conveniently opt out of participating in the study. The questionnaire was again discussed with a few executives who were not to be included in the final sample. The consensus of opinion indicated that the statements should be made single-edged and the response format should be reduced from seven to five points.

The statements in the original questionnaire were thus rewritten. It had the following composition:

Dimensions	No. of Statements
Innovation	4
Risk-taking	2
Proactivity	2
Futurity	5
Dynamism	5
Heterogeneity	4
Scanning	4
Technocratization	3
Differrentiation	3
Total	**32**

The rewritten statements were presented to a team of three senior executives. They were asked to discuss each statement for its comprehensibility, meaning, relevance to the situation prevalent in different types of industry and the response format. They suggested some changes in the language to make the response format more clear so that one category response could be clearly differentiated from the next category. These suggestions were incorporated in the questionnaire. Response categories of strongly agree, agree etc. were changed to agreement to below 20 per cent, 20–40 per cent etc. The revised questionnaire was again administered to six executives who were enrolled for a course in management at the local technology institute. The statements and response formats were found to be clear, yet a few more ambiguities were identified. Of the two statements included under innovation: (a) No new lines of product or service were marketed in the past five years; and (b) Changes in product lines have been mostly of a minor nature, it was decided to retain only the first one. It was recommended that the planning and forecasting activities under the heading of futurity should be treated as distinct activities and thus separate statements were written on them. The human resource development function was also added.

The final questionnaire consisted of a total of 35 items. This was pretested by administering it to a group of 10 senior executives in three different units. On most items the responses were clear, having an agreement of 80 per cent and above.

The final questionnaire was given to 300 seniormost managers in 20 public sector corporations and 50 managers in private sector enterprises. Of these a total number of 268 questionnaires in the public sector and 46 in the private sector were relevant. The scale items were averaged to obtain the aggregate scores. Cronbach Alpha was used as the construct reliability measure for all scales. These are reported in Table 3.1. The guideline of 0.80, established by Van de Ven and Ferry (1980) for measuring organizational attributes has been accepted. These are reported in Table 3.1.

Table 3.1: Cronbach Alphas for Different Variables

	Variable	Cronbach Alpha
1.	Strategy	
	1. Innovation	0.76
	2. Risk-taking	0.78
	3. Proactivity	0.89
	4. Futurity	0.74
2.	Environment	
	1. Dynamism	0.74
	2. Heterogeneity	0.78
3.	Structure	
	1. Scanning	0.79
	2. Technocratization	0.77
	3. Differentiation	0.82

Personal Orientation, Strategy-Making, Environment and Structure

Senior managers in general are inclined towards externality. It has been of little relevance to find out which sector a manager worked in or if the corporation made profits. The mean differences on personal orientation, between the private and public sectors, and between profit-and loss-making corporations, are not significant (Tables 3.2 and 3.3). Between the private and the public sectors, the managers do not differ significantly on any of the four strategies, perceptions of environment, and technocratization and differentiation aspects of structure. Managers in the two sectors vary significantly only on the scanning aspect of structure. The profit- and loss-making corporations differ significantly on the strategies of risk-taking and futurity, perceived heterogeneity in the environment, and technocratization.

Table 3.2: Means, Standard Deviations and 't' Values for Private and Public Sector Corporations on Measured Variables

Variables	Private sector		Public sector		
	Mean	SD	Mean	SD	't' Value
Internality–Externality	11.17	2.37	11.60	2.23	–
Innovation	9.83	1.97	9.36	2.45	–
Risk-taking	6.22	1.99	5.03	2.04	–
Proactivity	6.89	1.58	6.80	1.79	–
Futurity	24.63	4.31	24.16	5.55	–
Dynamism	15.54	2.96	15.79	3.67	–
Heterogeneity	11.76	2.88	11.42	3.12	–
Scanning	12.26	2.92	11.57	3.51	4.90**
Technocratization	6.00	1.59	5.85	1.75	–
Differentiation	9.65	2.13	9.06	2.90	–

** p<0.01

Table 3.3: Means, Standard Deviations and 't' Values for Profit- and Loss-making Public Sector Units on Measured Variables

Variables	Profit-Making		Loss-Making		
	Mean	SD	Mean	SD	't' Value
Internality–Externality	11.45	2.38	11.50	2.32	–
Innovation	9.35	2.38	9.38	2.55	–
Risk-taking	5.43	2.04	6.32	1.95	3.64**
Proactivity	6.89	1.78	6.71	1.81	–
Futurity	25.73	5.09	22.26	5.52	5.35**
Dynamism	15.93	3.96	15.67	3.43	–
Heterogeneity	11.06	3.25	11.86	2.90	2.10*
Scanning	11.68	3.70	11.45	3.29	–
Technocratization	5.59	1.80	6.17	1.63	2.75**
Differentiation	9.02	2.81	9.11	3.02	–

* p<0.05
** p<0.01

Managers in the profit-making corporations adopt more future-oriented strategies, while the strategy of risk taking is chosen more often in loss-making corporations. Managers in the loss- making corporations perceive the environment to be more heterogeneous and employ more technologists probably to control the losses. Managers in the public sector and loss-making corporations display a somewhat higher externality than those in the private sector and profit-making corporations. In one of their studies Miller et al. (1982) have reported a mean score of 5.54 and a standard deviation of 3.20 on chief executives. The lowest score in this group is 6 and the highest score is 18, in the expected range of 0-23. The groups are thus inclined towards externality.

The internality-oriented managers are only slightly more future-oriented in their choice of strategy (Table 3.4). The differences between internals and externals are not significant on any other dimension of strategy-making, perceptions of environment and structure. The internals score marginally higher on some variables and the externals score higher on other variables.

Table 3.4: Means, Standard Deviations and 't' Values for Public Sector Managers, Divided on Internality–Externality Score

Variables	Internality-Oriented		Externality-Oriented		
	Mean	SD	Mean	SD	't' Value
Innovation	9.40	2.47	9.33	2.44	–
Risk-taking	5.70	2.11	5.96	1.98	–
Proactivity	6.77	1.83	6.79	1.76	–
Futurity	24.84	5.39	23.54	5.64	1.84*
Dynamism	15.95	3.60	15.64	3.75	–
Heterogeneity	11.27	2.97	11.56	3.25	–
Scanning	11.81	3.54	11.36	3.49	–
Technocratization	5.84	1.58	5.86	1.89	–
Differentiation	9.34	2.80	8.81	2.99	–

* p<0.05

It has been researched that managers' personal orientations relate significantly to their corporate strategy-making, environment and structure. The correlations between personal orientation scores and strategy-making and between environment and structure for private and public sector groups and for profit-and loss-making corporations are included in Tables 3.5, 3.6, 3.7 and 3.8 respectively. The results do not really provide a positive answer. Most correlations are low and insignificant.

Table 3.5: Correlations among Strategy, Environment and Structure Variables in the Private Sector Group

Variables		I	RT	PA	F	D	H	S	T	Di	PO
I	Strategy	1.00									
RT		0.39**	1.00								
PA		0.27	0.04	1.00							
F		-0.08	-0.30**	0.42**	1.00						
D	Environ- ment	-0.00	-0.06	0.21	0.17	1.00					
H		-0.10	-0.38**	0.19	-0.31*	-0.14	1.00				
S	Structure	-0.10	-0.18	0.34**	0.58**	0.18	-0.16	1.00			
T		0.12	0.38**	0.28	0.08	0.08	-0.02	0.09	1.00		
Di		0.03	-0.22	0.17	0.01	0.10	0.02	0.21	0.01	1.00	
PO		-0.09	0.21	-0.26	-0.06	0.13	0.12	-0.12	0.09	0.15	1.00

* $p<0.05$
** $p<0.01$

I=Innovation; RT=Risk-taking; PA=Proactivity; F=Futurity; D=Dynamism; H=Heterogeneity; S=Scanning; T=Technocratization; Di=Differentiation; PO=Personal orientation.

Table 3.6: Correlations among Strategy, Environment and Structure Variables in the Public Sector Group

Variables		I	RT	PA	F	D	H	S	T	Di	PO
I	Strategy	1.00									
RT		0.15*	1.00								
PA		0.32**	0.19**	1.00							
F		0.26**	0.03	0.42**	1.00						
D	Environment	0.22**	0.14*	0.30**	0.19**	1.00					
H		0.19*	0.27**	0.18**	0.10	0.37**	1.00				
S	Structure	0.33**	0.10	0.36**	0.40**	0.23**	0.11	1.00			
T		0.08	0.06	0.23*	0.10	0.07	0.15*	0.12	1.00		
Di		0.21**	0.05	0.11	0.18**	0.22**	0.18**	0.20**	0.12	1.00	
PO		-0.04	-0.11	-0.07	0.10	0.05	-0.09	-0.06	-0.07	-0.10	1.00

* $p<0.05$
** $p<0.01$

I=Innovation; RT=Risk-taking; PA=Proactivity; F=Futurity; D=Dynamism; H=Heterogeneity; S=Scanning; T=Technocratization; Di=Differentiation; PO=Personal orientation.

Table 3.7: **Correlations among Strategy, Environment and Structure Variables in the Profit-Making Group**

Variables		I	RT	PA	F	D	H	S	T	Di	PO
I		1.00									
RT	Stra-	0.19*	1.00								
PA	tegy	0.31**	0.19*	1.00							
F		0.18*	0.14	0.32**	1.00						
D	Envi-	0.26**	0.00	0.25**	0.12	1.00					
H	ron-	0.11	0.23**	0.14	0.19*	0.32**	1.00				
	ment										
S		0.32**	0.15	0.28**	0.34**	0.27**	0.13	1.00			
T	Struc-	0.14	0.03	0.26**	0.25**	0.13	0.13	0.12	1.00		
Di	ture	0.25**	0.11	0.14	0.24**	0.27**	0.23**	0.18*	0.16*	1.00	
PO		-0.07	0.14	0.08	-0.08	-0.07	0.02	-0.02	0.12	-0.20*	1.00

* $p<0.05$
** $p<0.01$

I=Innovation; RT=Risk-taking; PA=Proactivity; F=Futurity; D=Dynamism; H=Heterogeneity; S=Scanning; T=Technocratization; Di=Differentiation; PO=Personal orientation.

Table 3.8: **Correlations among Strategy, Environment and Structure Variables in the Loss-Making Group**

Variables		I	RT	PA	F	D	H	S	T	Di	PO
I		1.00									
RT	Stra-	0.09	1.00								
PA	tegy	0.33**	0.22*	1.00							
F		0.38**	0.20*	0.54**	1.00						
D	Envi-	0.18*	0.29**	0.35**	0.29**	1.00					
H	ron-	0.28**	0.28**	0.24**	0.10	0.49**	1.00				
	ment										
S		0.35**	0.13	0.46**	0.50**	0.19*	0.09	1.00			
T	Struc-	0.08	0.10	0.21*	0.06	-0.01	0.13	0.15	1.00		
Di	ture	0.18*	0.23**	0.07	0.14	0.17*	0.12	0.23**	0.06	1.00	
PO		0.08	0.16*	0.04	-0.08	-0.12	0.05	-0.08	0.14	-0.03	1.00

* $p<0.05$
** $p<0.01$

I=Innovation; RT=Risk-taking; PA=Proactivity; F=Futurity; D=Dynamism; H=Heterogeneity; S=Scanning; T=Technocratization; Di=Differentiation; PO=Personal orientation.

In the private sector group, although the personal orientation of managers has a positive relationship with risk-taking and proactive strategies, it is not significantly related to any of the two variables, indicating that corporate strategy-making, environment and structure may be largely independent of the personal orientation of managers.

The externality of public sector managers is associated with the choice of futurity strategy, although the correlation is not significant. The externals used future-oriented strategies more than the internals. This finding has been in the expected direction, but it may only be true to the extent that the externals would ensure that their actions lead to expected outcomes. The advantage of the externals over the internals consists in their inherent tendency of information collection and its utilization in the given situation, but if they find that the situation is complex and tightly constrained by extraneous factors (as inevitable in the public sector and quite likely in private sector enterprises), their future outcomes and subsequent expectations may not be different from those of the internals. It can be argued that externality is not necessarily a negative attribute. According to Levinson (1980) this has been found advantageous for people whose perceptions of control by powerful others are realistic because of the specific situations they are in. As such, many of the senior managers have little control over the decision-making processes. They perceive their roles as tools of implementation rather than as decisionmakers. The internality-oriented managers are able to take more risks only marginally. In fact, if the direction of relationship is used as an indicator of corporate strategy-making, then it is noticed that the internals use risky, innovative and proactive strategies less than the externals.

The personal orientation of the public sector managers is associated with the differentiation aspect of structure. The internality of managers has been slightly higher in industries which have diverse structures and product types. The access to diverse structures and products helps managers in acquiring increased security, control and confidence. The sense of greater control through diversification is an external contingency, but it probably helped in sustaining profits or avoiding losses, and was thus of personal significance to managers.

The personal orientation of managers has a low relationship with strategy-making, perceptions of environment and structure variables in the public and private sectors. Also the relationships are in different directions. When comparing the two sectors, the differences in the direction of relationships of personal orientation of managers to strategy-making, perceptions of environment and structure indicate differences in the contextual pressures, location of sectors in the socio-economic structure, objectives, organizational structures and networks etc. While the private sector managers scoring towards internality can take more risks (if they wish to) and work actively, in the public sector the managers taking more risk do so under extraneous pressures and thus score towards externality. In general, in the former group, it is the internality of managers that is associated with risk-taking and proactive strategies, while in the latter group the externality dimension facilitates the choice of these two strategies. The public sector presents to the managers a situation of a no gain or no loss at the personal level. The situation happens to be different in the case of the private sector, where managers are required to take risks even as individuals. In both cases, internality helps in the adoption of innovative strategy, and externality affects the future orientation. The private sector managers find externality useful in the enactment of and the coping with a dynamic and heterogeneous environment, but the public sector managers' internality helps them in dealing with the heterogeneous elements in the business environ- ment. Internals prefer to have scanning done much more routinely and look for diversified structures in both sets of corporations.

Managers in the private sector have relatively more flexibility in the choice of strategy than do managers in the public sector. This makes them adventurous, confident, assertive and active, and thus more inclined to use risk-taking and proactive strategies. They prefer to work through the problems they confront rather than leave the outcome to chance or to others. They habitually spend their time thinking about doing things, rather than waiting for instructions from outside, or allowing the solution to emerge in a natural sequence. The public sector managers who are inflexible, worrying, methodical, rigid, anachronistic and overly deferential to authority have an ab- horrence for risk-taking. The large public sector enterprises tend to reinforce a more bureaucratized orientation in managers and thus the consequent externality. The strategy of innovation is positively related to the complementary strategies of risk-taking, proactivity and futurity according to Miller et al. (1982). Risk-taking embraces probability of failure. Proactive managers are found generating pres- sure on others to act in a similar direction. Some managers undertake futuristic planning more as a natural activity than others. Miller et al. (1982) have observed that internal executives are more likely to engage in strategies that are proactive, risky and involve planning for the future. They are more given to tailor their enterprises to different circumstances as needed for better performance in dynamic environments.

In the two sectors, managers as individuals have different choices and inclinations open to them, and thus choose to take risks in different ways. Such findings have been reported in some experimental studies (Cohen, Jaffray and Said, 1985), but the evidence from organizational studies has been either weak or missing. Many experts on decision-making indeed believe that there is no individual inclination of a high generality to take risks of a certain magnitude (Dahlback, 1990).

An explanation of these somewhat unexpected findings has been found inherent in the location of public enterprises in the Indian socio-political structures and the position of seniormost managers within them. The public sector in India is highly regarded, but its autonomy remains a misnomer. The public sector has to function under the directives of the related ministries of the Government of India, making the position of managers/technocrats subordinate to the bureaucrats. It also has to cope with the need to achieve the socio-economic objectives and to deal with a variety of external controls. Managers who can be successfully manipulated by political and bureaucratic forces in the context, and also keep their personal feelings to themselves, are found extrinsically motivated to take more risks and demonstrate activity-orientation of a higher degree. Conversely, managers who tend to act at their own initiative, conviction and confidence find external controls inhibitive and demotivating. They take little or no risks and are not activity-oriented.

In profit-making corporations the personal orientation of managers is found significantly related to differentiated structures. The internals are able to cope better with diverse structures. They are slightly more innovative and futuristic and deal with dynamic environments effectively, but externals take more risks and are more proactive. The more technically qualified are relatively more externality-oriented, suggesting that their professional expertise made them more active in their search for cues in business environments. The personal orientation of managers in loss-making corporations is not significantly related with any aspects of strategy, environment and structure. Some relationships are however worth considering. The externals take substantial risks and adopt innovative strategies, but the internals are more futuristic. The internals cope with dynamic environments in a better way and scan more routinely. The technically qualified are more external in this group also.

Managers in loss-making corporations attempt to take more risks but fail to actively respond to the variety of challenges in the environment than those in profit-making corporations. This finding, along with the sectoral observations, indicates that the public sector and profit-making corporations respond to the environmental variety, complexity and dynamics in more subtle ways. This has similarity to the observation of Boyd (1990) that the high performing firms are more responsive to environmental uncertainty. The situation is relatively more difficult for the managers in the loss-making group, as for them a no-response situation also turns into a poor-response situation and is discounted.

There are similarities as well as differences between profit-and loss-making corporations. The externals, in general, have higher technical qualifications and take more risks, while the internals are more future-oriented and are better prepared to cope with turbulent and challenging environments. A greater use of innovative strategy has been made by internality-oriented in profit-making corporations, and by externality-oriented in loss-making corporations.

Managers of loss-making corporations and in private sector take slightly higher risks, often even as compulsions. Similarly, externals take higher risks even if non-significant, as they find the management of contextual factors a necessity. The finding that the loss-making group and the private sector group of managers have a slightly higher mean on perceived heterogeneity in the environment than the profit-making group and the public sector group of managers indicates that the former are more responsive to variety in the environment. The public sector and particularly the profit-making group of managers deal with environmental dynamism somewhat better.

Internals are expected to take more risks than externals as they see themselves strong as individuals. However, the finding that internals use a little more of the risk taking strategy in the public sector has another connotation. They do so (if such is the case) because of the extraneous condition that their jobs are quite secure. The finding that externals in the private sector and loss-making groups use the risk-taking strategy relatively more precisely confirms this, as they perceive the management of contextual factors like job retention as a necessary condition of their functioning.

The use of the risk-taking strategy requires that managers should have some a priori idea about the rewards accruing in case of success/ profits, and whether these can be considered greater than the consequences of failure/losses. The expected does not always happen, however. The risks of decision-making are much lower for managers as individuals in the public sector than for their counterparts in the private sector, and less in the profit- than in the loss-making group. In the public sector, at the most, as individuals they can be mauled, transferred, and not promoted, but in the private sector they can even lose their jobs, without having the opportunity to explain, reconsider or act on their failures.

The congruence between the personality dispositions of managers, their strategy-making and their perceptions of environment and structure may be theoretically quite relevant to the outcomes, but in reality it seems to be largely constrained and organization-based. The public sector corporations in India have been set up with specific objectives and the government exercises control through policies of recruitment, pricing, tariffs, credits and technology imports/development, resource allocation, location of plants etc. This has made the managers highly dependent on the government and induced in them a sense of passivity and powerlessness.

It was expected, following the congruence theory, that the organizations would create climates in which managers will learn to grab opportunities—'take, yield and adjust'—and thus evolve a functional congruence between their personal needs and goals and the organizations' needs and goals. This has been true only to some extent as the managers interviewed felt that equity, ownership and other organizational and environmental attributes in the enterprises have been so controlled and circumvented that little discretion is left to them as individuals. This finding has been different from the findings of Miller et al. (1982, 1986) who found the chief executives' locus of control directly linked to the choice of strategy and indirectly related to the perceptions of environment and structure. Kets de Vries and Miller (1984) have argued that the structures in organizations are reflections of the personalities of the chief executive officers. The findings are, however, quite relevant from the perspective of the Indian social and corporate contextual reality. The hypothesis of contextual influences on strategic decisions has also been supported by Bateman and Zeithaml (1989).

Strategy-Making, Environment and Structure

Some significant associations were expected among the dimensions of strategy and the perceptions of environment and structure, and this has been found true to a considerable extent. In the private sector, innovation is significantly related to risk-taking, although it has a positive correlation also with the proactivity strategy. The risk-taking strategy is negatively associated with the futurity strategy, and positively associated with the perceptions of heterogeneity in the environment, technocratization and differentiation aspects of structure. The risk-taking strategy can be used by managers for obtaining immediate success, but in fact the technically qualified managers adopt this strategy to deal with the heterogeneous elements in the environment on a long-term basis. Highly proactive managers are more futurity-oriented, have higher technical skills and scan the available information more frequently as a routine. Futurity- oriented managers make frequent use of scanning structures, yet they do not always feel comfortable in a heterogeneous environment. A successful coping with the variety of challenges requires them to use the scanning structures more than those at the surface level. Managers who have external orientations cope better with turbulent environments, and relate to diversified structures somewhat more effectively than the internals. This finding has not been in the expected direction, but appears to be quite pragmatic in the prevalent business context in India.

Public sector managers who use the innovation strategy also adopt the risk-taking, proactivity and futurity strategies. They perceive dynamism and variety in the environment, and prefer the scanning aspect of structure (Table 3.6). Innovation, activity-orientation and planning are relevant in dynamic environments and in corporations having expanding structures. Managers in private firms are more proactive, cope better with uncertainty and maintain their customers according to Anderson, Hellriegel and Slocum (1977). Theoretically, the use of the innovation strategy should require that enterprises recruit more technocrats and professionally trained managers, but this is not universally true. In the public sector the intent and capability to innovate of even technically qualified managers gets reduced over the years by the continued use of external controls. The use of the risk-taking strategy and the recruitment of technocrats emerges important in

the private sector, where managers have limited day-to-day interference in their functioning, have opportunities of using their technical
skills and doing different things, and where turnaround can be
achieved. The control type and the profit status of the enterprises
thus appears to determine the nature of relationship among strategy-
making, environment and structure.

The innovation strategy has not correlated significantly with the
technocratization aspect of structure in public sector, however. Neither
are the managers required to introduce and invent novel products
and alternatives, nor are the professionals (engineers and scientists)
assigned overriding special roles in the decision-making process.
The risk-taking strategy does not correlate significantly with futurity
or any aspect of the structure. Evidently, managers do not take any
risks to improve planning, to identify shifts in the needs of clients/
markets, to use the variety of technologies and to widen the range
of existing products. Some risks are inherent in the innovations and
activities that managers might undertake as well as in the sustenance
of activities in the environments which are dynamic and heterogeneous. Proactivity correlates with futurity, dynamism correlates
with heterogeneity in the environment, and the scanning aspect correlates with the technocratization aspect of structure. The activity-
conscious managers undertake planning, are more dynamic, and choose
the needed technology from the available range. The futurity strategy
correlates significantly with dynamism in the environment, but not
with heterogeneity, indicating that futurity-oriented managers enact
dynamic environments for themselves, but not necessarily of the
heterogeneous type, even though the aspects of dynamism and heterogeneity of the environment correlate significantly with each other.

A few more relations among the variables are significant in the
public sector and profit-making corporations, than in the private
sector and the loss-making corporations. In the profit-making corporations all the four types of strategy are found operative together
(Table 3.7), but in the loss-making corporations the innovation strategy
is only minimally associated with risk-taking. The innovation strategy
correlates significantly with the aspect of dynamism of the environment in the profit-making group, but with dynamism as well as
heterogeneity in the loss-making group. In both groups it is significantly associated with the aspects of scanning and differentiation
of structure. Risk-taking is used along with the proactivity strategy
in both the groups, but with futurity in the loss-making group only.

It affects the perceptions of heterogeneity in the environment of the profit-making group, and the two aspects of the environment and the differentiation aspect of structure in the loss-making group. The proactivity strategy is used with futurity in the profit-making group, but is used even more in the loss-making group. Yet strategies can be used to different extents by the two groups. The proactivity strategy is positively associated with both aspects of the environment, and scanning and technocratization aspects of structure in both the groups. The futurity strategy is significantly used in heterogeneous environments and with all types of structure in the profit-making group, but only in relation to the aspect of scanning of structure in the loss-making group.

Dynamism in environment is found associated with the scanning and differentiation aspects of structure in both groups, while heterogeneity correlates with differentiation in the profit-making group. Dynamic environments require constant monitoring, acceptance of the new range of technology and expansion of the range of current activities. The three aspects of structure are found interdependent, although only scanning has significant correlation with differentiation. A knowledge of shifts in market, etc., is not sufficient to stimulate the search for and the use of new technology.

Dynamism and heterogeneity in the environment operate together to a significant extent, indicating that both groups find the presence of changing and diverse elements in the environment exciting. Dynamism in the environment is found to encourage the use of scanning and differentiated structures, indicating that successful coping with changing environments requires all corporations to make use of scanning as well as diversified structures. Diversification in structures in profit-making corporations is found operative when appropriate scanning has been done, and there are an adequate number of scientists and technologists working to cope with the variety of challenges. Loss-making corporations can diversify on the basis of scanning mechanism.

Some Inferences

The present findings are somewhat different from the earlier ones in which some common configurations among strategic, environmental and structural variables have been identified (Miles and Snow,

1978, Mintzberg, 1978; and Miller and Friesen, 1984). The significant interdependence of aspects of the environment and structure demonstrate that environmental dynamism and heterogeneity together make management tasks more complex and uncertain. Dealing with such environments often requires that different structures are used in different settings. Examples are: less formalized and more flexible structures in the private sector (Burns and Stalker, 1961), a diverse array of departments and roles of the public sector type (Lawrence and Lorsch, 1967), and more intensive face-to-face liaison devices to promote collaboration 'and resolve differences (Galbraith, 1973) in both sectors. Such structures would improve the environment and facilitate more power delegation based on task specialization that would give recognition to the technical skills.

In the context of developing economies, Kim (1980) has observed that innovation is essential for organizations to survive and grow in a competitive environment. This requires a high level of knowledge and expertise and supporting structural variables. It has been recognized also by managers in the private sector as well as in the public sector that in an uncertain and changing environment, diversity and professional skills can bring a variety of information to encourage the use of the innovation strategy, and can be used to facilitate a recognition of need/opportunity. Organizations should provide managers room for discretion and freedom in dealing with undefined and changing situations. Rigid rules and procedures limit them to become aware of potential markets and technical opportunities. These are also detrimental to the generation of creative ideas and their implementation.

Similar arguments have been advanced by some other researchers in India and elsewhere. Ramamurthi (1982) has compared the performance of two public sector enterprises in India attached to the same ministry and has observed that the superior performance of some enterprises is related to buoyancy in the market, which is an extraneous variable. Researchers have also reported significant relationships between certain aspects of the environment and the mode of management as these together affect the performance (Khandwalla, 1977, 1983). In a study of public and private sector managers, it has been observed that public sector managers rank good industrial relations significantly higher in importance and coping with environmental changes much lower in importance than do private sector managers (FORE, 1984). The turbulent and threatening environments require management of an entrepreneurial type, and professional management is more suitable in a complex environment. Environmental turbulence is found largely uncontrollable, and a major constraint on performance (Cameron, 1986b). Khandwalla (1984) has observed that innovation in an organization is affected by a turbulent operating environment, resource scarcity, vulnerability due to inexperience, competition, calculated risk-taking, strong result orientation, vigorous environmental scanning for opportunities, good control and information systems and opportunistic diversification. The use of innovation strategy would necessarily be contingent on other strategies as well as on environmental and structural variables. Technology has been found related to strategy and is important in improving performance, as it can actually alter the structures (Willard and Cooper, 1985), and affect competitive advantage (Porter, 1985). It can also be useful in inducing innovation and vertical integration (Balakrishnan and Wernerfelt, 1986).

Overall, managers are inclined towards externality. The sectoral identity has been important only in the scanning aspect of structure. The profit status of corporations facilitates the varied use of the risk-taking and futurity strategies, the heterogeneity aspect of the environment, and the technocratization aspect of structure. The personal orientation of managers fails to show any marked association with the choice of strategy and perceptions of environment and structure, but numerous other significant relationships emerge in all groups and are useful.

Irrespective of the sector and the profit status of corporations, the personality of the managers remains subservient to organizational and environmental factors. As individuals the managers feel insecure, insignificant and powerless particles of humanity in which their actions have little meaning. They do not strive for challenge and excellence and tend to accept the status quo. Once the managers are recruited, they are expected to adapt and mold themselves into the organizational culture, whether soft or synergetic. The organizational processes are influenced by the outside social milieu which remains the same for the two sectors, and thus result in similar organizational socialization, whereby managers are pushed towards externality. Externality has been observed to be a general characteristic of Indians at all levels by Kanungo (1990). Whatever may be the inner strength of managers, decision-making gets guided by extraneous considerations, as the resources lie in the social domain. This seems to provide support to the argument of Bandura (1986) that in the transactions of everyday life, an individual's beliefs regarding self-efficacy and controllability of the environment are not divorced from experiential realities. Rather, the beliefs are products of reciprocal causation. Another source of variation is found inherent in the selection process by which more internal ones get sorted out at the entry point itself and are lost to the organized systems. It has been suggested by Spector (1982) that locus of control may be a useful variable in employee selection, as it would relate to many aspects of behaviour in the organizations. This ought to be experimented first and reasoned out carefully before being accepted in the Indian set-up.

4

TIME MANAGEMENT

Time and Managers

Time is a resource, which gets depleted constantly, and often without one being aware of it. It is axiomatic that work expands to fill the time slotted for it. High achievers function under stringent time pressures, while low achievers do not necessarily give adequate time to their activities. When one wants to achieve, even if one is hard-pressed for time, one learns to use every minute judiciously.

The way in which managers manage their time across different activities at work and other aspects of life has been of central importance in the modern industrial sector. In fact, on this rests the existence and survival of most corporations. Since the publication of Lakein's (1973) book *How to get control of your time and your life*, numerous writings have emphasized the virtues of efficient time management in the life of a person in different organized settings. Many consultants recommend that one must identify one's needs and wants, prioritize them in terms of importance and then allocate one's time and resources judiciously to be able to achieve optimal efficiency. Management manuals have been in use in some organizations and improvements have been reported. Poor time management behaviours have often been talked about as a source of stress and poor performance (Gall, 1988; Longman and Atkinson, 1988).

It has been argued that effective time management is synonymous with effective management. It is central to economies of effort and resources in all organizations, whether they are government controlled or private. This seems to be particularly relevant for Indian industry, which has been chronically plagued by time and cost overruns leading to wasteful expenditure and losses. There is an urgent need to train managers in alternative techniques of time management and socialize them in the value of effective time management behaviours.

How does one distribute one's time over different life activities on an average day? How does one distribute one's work time over different job activities? These questions are the crux of the problem of effective/ineffective management. Time management has been included in this study as a variable, although many systematic studies could not be located to provide an empirical rationale. The Spanish study, known as the *Work Importance Study* (WIS) and recorded by de Lecea (1982), has included the variable of time distribution on the five major life roles; and this has been used with some modification by Sinha (1988) in his study of work culture in Indian organizations.

Time Management—Concept and Measurement

Time management has been conceptualized as a composite of (*a*) time distribution on various life activities on an average day; (*b*) work time allocation, and (*c*) work overload.

Time Distribution

It has been said more often than not that if managers could distribute their time judiciously over different activities that are related to their life and implicit in their multiple roles, and observe this distribution of time, there would be little scope for inefficiencies at the personal or corporate level. They would be happy and satisfied as individuals, and their unit would be able to make optimal use of time and other resources.

The Spanish team of the WIS group (de Lecea, 1982) has developed a time distribution scale, which measures how managers distribute their time of 24 hours on various activities related to their life. Following this scale six areas have been included in this study, namely: family (like taking care of the house, dependents and shopping obligations etc.); hobbies (taking time out for activities that really interest them and give them pleasure, such as: music, dancing, swimming and reading etc.); social (meeting, helping, entertaining and visiting friends and relations, discharging social obligations); work (undertake job related activities that give pay, promotion and status); sleeping and personal care (satisfying biological, hygiene and grooming needs) and others (unexpected engagements and irregular activities like neighbourhood meetings, community activities etc.). This is similar to the conceptualization of family, leisure and work, as reported by Knowles and Taylor (1990), among managers of information technology. A question was formulated for managers, asking them to divide their time of 24 hours of an average day under six activity types, namely, family, hobbies, social, work, sleeping and personal care and others. The Cronbach Alpha on the measure was 0.94.

Work Time Allocation

Once the managers had given the information on the time distribution for an average work-day, they were asked to indicate how they divided their time over various work activities. This was done by specifying the amount of time over the list of nine work-roles which encompassed major work activities at the senior managerial level. This procedure was expected to inform the researcher about the self-consistency of managers to the extent that the total work time would equal the sum of time spent on all these activities. Secondly, the distribution of such responses should be indicative of the modal work profile of the seniormost managers in the public and private enterprises. It has a Cronbach Alpha of 0.85.

Work Overload

The frequency with which managers extend work to their homes should indicate extra work demands made on them, either because of their own inadequacy or as a result of the inadequacies of the organizational procedures. This has been measured by one item having three possible choices. The higher frequency of work taken home has been taken as indicative of a higher workload.

Time Management Profiles

General

The actual time distribution on an average work-day in the life of a manager should inform us about the dispersion and spacing of time across different roles played at home, at work and in society. However, two inherent difficulties should be kept in view: (a) The statutory regulation of work-time makes it a systemic variable, and yet in practice it can be used by role occupants differentially; (b) the time spent on work may not necessarily indicate the intensity with which the time is utilized for work activities. There may be significant inter-sector and inter-unit variations, and yet these may not be necessarily related to either the quantity of task accomplishment or to the quality of work.

The two major activities on which most managers spend nearly three-fourths of the total 24 hours (17-18 hours) are work and sleeping and personal care. The mean scores on time spent on work range between 8.25 and 10.47 hours, given the fact that the organizations have the statutory requirement of 8.00 to 8.30 working hours on a work-day. On sleeping and personal care, the time spent ranges between 6.75 and 8.50 hours.

On an average managers spend time close to 2.50 hours on family-related activities. The time given to hobbies by managers ranged from 25 minutes to one hour and 45 minutes a day.

The time spent by managers on work encompassed a variety of activities, namely, discussions with superiors; discussions with juniors and peers; planning and managing; paperwork; sitting in meetings; taking inspection rounds of offices and factories; sorting out matters with ministry officials; obtaining information about market trends and other unscheduled activities. It has been interesting to observe that approximately 92.50 per cent of managers add their time distribution correctly, equal to the time spent on work. They show thus a great deal of intra-individual consistency as well as an awareness of the utilization of time. They show a good cognitive balance in the planning and management of time.

Sectoral

The subtle differences in the time charts of private and public sectors reflect on the differences in the systems of governance. The Indian state has adopted the socialist welfare model of governance (a 'soft' state), in which the prevalent economic, political and social structure determine the nature of plans, policies and practices. A 'soft' state, as observed by Myrdal (1968), is reluctant to put its populace under any compulsion and thus is unable to induce a sense of discipline among its people. The soft system of governance does not provide precise or even good definitions of commitments, assurances and work expectations. This model of governance has been accepted in the political arena and has pervaded all organizational systems, whether fully or partially controlled by the state. Most public sector enterprises, central and state government undertakings, today are blessed with the soft model of governance and management, and are unable to cultivate the value of time even at sufficiently higher levels.

The privately controlled and managed enterprises, on the other hand, demand and enforce on its members norms of high productivity, higher capacity utilization, punctuality, efficiency and profits, while a workable emphasis is placed on the welfare of the employees. In the private sector responsibilities are clearly delineated and lapses are not taken lightly. Indiscipline at the managerial level elicits prompt action. Organizations maintain by and large normative power structures. They have thus some of the attributes of a synergetic culture.

The two kinds of governance and managements generate different kinds of working conditions, management, employee attitudes and commitment affecting day-to-day work life, rewards and performance, and thus work culture. This has been the expectation and the reality to some extent.

Managers in the private and public sectors (synergetic versus soft) have their origin in the same social group, and show overriding effects of the social milieu and statutory provisions, but some variations in time management patterns are noted, though not significant (Table 4.1). Managers in the public sector tend to give more time to unscheduled emergencies and irregular activities. The time schedules of private sector managers are found much more tightly packed, leaving little room for indulgence in irrelevant activities. Managers in the private sector spend less time (about half an hour) on these activities in a day than those in the public sector. Further, managers tend to distribute their time on work-related activities somewhat differently. These differences are meaningful in terms of sectoral identities and social milieu.

Table 4.1: *Means, Standard Deviations and 't' Values on Time Distribution and Allocation for Private and Public Sector Corporations*

Variables	Private sector		Public sector		
	Mean	SD	Mean	SD	't' Value
Family	2.61	1.36	2.65	1.31	–
Hobbies	0.96	0.99	1.12	0.91	–
Social life	1.33	0.99	1.30	0.78	–
Work	9.93	1.10	9.69	1.47	–
Sleeping and personal care	7.98	1.88	7.81	1.41	–
Others	0.74	1.12	1.20	1.16	2.50*
Superiors	1.67	1.10	1.27	0.68	3.35**
Juniors and peers	1.70	1.17	1.66	0.89	–
Planning and managing	1.39	0.88	1.66	1.02	–
Paperwork	1.04	0.82	1.80	1.28	3.87**
Meetings	1.22	0.94	1.32	0.90	–
Rounds	0.83	0.93	0.57	0.64	2.29*
Ministry work	0.54	0.75	0.44	0.61	–
Market trends	1.37	1.73	0.58	0.64	5.61**
Others	1.20	1.80	0.58	0.83	3.73**
Work overload	2.43	0.91	2.01	0.78	3.33**

* p<0.05
** p<0.01

It has been observed that managers in the private sector spend during the work-day more time (about half an hour) than their counterparts in the public sector on discussions with superiors, 15-16 minutes more in taking inspection rounds of offices and factories, nearly 45 minutes more in knowing the market trends, and about 35 minutes more in miscellaneous activities. The public sector managers spend during one work-day nearly 46 minutes more on paperwork than managers in the private sector. The other non-significant and differentiating activities on which the public sector managers spend relatively more time than the private sector managers are planning and managing meetings. These are given much importance as rituals in the public sector, but not much outcome is either expected or results from them.

While core work activities are accorded some primacy over peripheral (supportive) activities in the private sector, the opposite is the case in the public sector. Paperwork and small irrelevant activities (like organizing parties for visitors of the concerned ministry, and going to meet officials on their calls whether they have any purpose or not) take a substantial amount of the work time of public sector managers. The four activities, namely, taking rounds, knowing about market trends, sorting out with ministry officials and other activities are given little time in all the units. Most managers spend a large proportion of their work time on discussions, meetings, planning and managing and paperwork. In terms of categorizing the activities as core and peripheral, evidently more managerial time goes into peripheral activities. This perhaps defines the nature of managerial jobs at the seniormost level in the corporations. Managers have to act as bureaucrats along with the technical jobs they do. Additionally, they are expected to act as subtle human links in the organizational hierarchy, they have to absorb the shocks from within the organizations and from the environment outside, and they have to keep the organizations going. This is the modal profile of senior managers.

Most managerial jobs are known to include a component of work overload, and more so at the senior level. In fact, it has been frequently stated by most chairmen/managing directors during the discussions that, in high managerial jobs, most people are involved in work every minute of their life. Whether at office or at home they are always preoccupied with work, they are over-committed on time, and they routinely (as a matter of habit) spend extra time on the job. However, the statement has not found empirical support. Managers seem to exaggerate the extra time spent on work. The extra amount of time a manager spent has not been more than three hours per week in any case, although they psychologically feel so. However, there has been no unit where managers have reported not spending extra time. If managers are under physical or mental pressure/stress at work, it is not really the work as such. What exists perhaps is a strong generalized tendency of feeling psychologically ambivalent. They tend to prolong the actual work hours by extending even the small amount of work to home-office-home and always feel that the work is pending.

Private sector managers take work home much more frequently than public sector managers. Many managers in the private sector report that indeed it is expected of them, and this has often been rewarded implicitly or explicitly. Public sector managers report taking work home less frequently, as they have limited freedom of action in their respective positions and it may invite the wrath of their bosses in the ministry concerned. Besides it is not seen in a positive light by their own colleagues.

Profit Status

The profit status of the corporation matters to some extent in time management (Table 4.2). Managers in the profit- making corporations spend approximately 36 minutes more on daily work. They spend relatively more time on planning and managing (approximately 28 minutes more in a day), as planning according to them happens to be the crux of corporate performance. Planning includes resource identification/generation, mobilization, allocation, identification of manpower needs, foreseeing environmental constraints etc. They also spend time more intensively. They spend extra time on the work more frequently, as they take work home almost every day, against two or three times by managers in the loss-making corporations. Managers in the loss-making corporations spend more time on discussions with superiors (often on demand from the chairmen and bosses in the concerned ministry), who consider it their sacred duty to give repeated instructions regarding rules, kind of management, relations among colleagues, losses (negative feedback), completing paperwork (as keeping detailed records lends to personal credibility and job security) and unspecified activities, which may only be of trivial importance to the work. They spend time on these activities more out of the compulsions of their position in the corporation. They are there because they are trapped and not because they chose to be there. They are required to seek the approval of their corporate bosses and the ministry concerned even on trivial things and these opportunities are often used by the latter to make them feel small and incompetent at the individual level, and non-performing and demoralized at the corporate level. The government authorities have little genuine concern for the time losses suffered by the corporations, but have a good deal of interest in tightening the controls.

Table 4.2: Means, Standard Deviations and 't' Values on Time Distribution and Allocation for Profit- and Loss-Making Public Sector Corporations

Variables	Profit-Making		Loss-Making		
	Mean	SD	Mean	SD	't' Value
Family	2.64	1.28	2.66	1.36	–
Hobbies	1.10	0.91	1.14	0.91	–
Social life	1.33	0.79	1.26	0.77	–
Work	9.92	1.44	9.41	1.47	2.88**
Sleeping and personal care	7.96	1.56	7.97	1.20	–
Others	1.12	1.16	1.30	1.15	–
Superiors	1.21	0.64	1.34	0.73	–
Juniors and peers	1.75	0.93	1.56	0.85	–
Planning and managing	1.82	0.98	1.48	0.50	2.71**
Paperwork	1.76	1.34	1.86	1.22	–
Meetings	1.38	0.95	1.24	0.84	–
Rounds	0.59	0.65	0.55	0.63	–
Ministry work	0.49	0.65	0.38	0.57	–
Market trends	0.63	0.66	0.52	0.61	–
Others	0.55	0.79	0.63	0.88	–
Work overload	2.11	0.80	1.89	0.73	2.29*

* $p < 0.05$
** $p < 0.01$

Personal Orientation

Managers oriented to internality or to externality show some differences in time management and distribution (Table 4.3). Although the differences are not significant, the internals manage to spend more time with the family as well as on work, particularly in holding meetings and keeping abreast of market trends. The externals manage to give a little more time in the area of unspecified activities (approximately 10 minutes more per day). The internals spend relatively more time on discussions with juniors and peers (about 14 minutes more per day). Managers who feel that their actions are controlled by external forces in the environment spend more time on trivial, unorganized activities and emergencies, while those who feel they control their own actions spend more time in meeting family obligations and job responsibilities. They take pleasure in meeting these demands and are able to cope with challenges in different spheres of life. Managers oriented to internality derive their strength and satisfaction from their discussions with peers and juniors and thus enjoy group support. They find such meetings to be positive windows to the outside world. They provide opportunities that help them to collect a variety of information and to identify the ways in which to use it. They collect data on market trends (needs, preferences of clients, competitors etc.) regularly in order to develop their own as well as corporate- level preparedness for making timely adaptation to the required changes.

Table 4.3: Means, Standard Deviations and 't' Values on Time Distribution and Allocation for Managers of the Public Sector Corporations, divided on Internality–Externality Score

Variables	Internality-Oriented		Externality-Oriented		
	Mean	SD	Mean	SD	't' Value
Family	2.78	1.32	2.53	1.30	–
Hobbies	1.10	0.88	1.14	0.94	–
Social life	1.27	0.84	1.33	0.72	–
Work	9.79	1.41	9.59	1.52	–
Sleeping and personal care	7.71	1.53	7.91	1.29	–
Others	1.11	1.14	1.28	1.17	2.06*
Superiors	1.21	0.69	1.32	0.67	–
Juniors and peers	1.78	1.00	1.56	0.78	2.08*
Planning and managing	1.72	1.14	1.61	0.90	–
Paperwork	1.78	1.40	1.82	1.17	–
Meetings	1.34	0.98	1.29	0.83	–
Rounds	0.59	0.66	0.56	0.63	–
Ministry work	0.41	0.60	0.46	0.63	–
Market trends	0.63	0.64	0.54	0.64	–
Others	0.60	0.83	0.57	0.83	–
Work overload	2.03	0.80	1.99	0.75	–

* $p < 0.05$

It has been observed by Macan, Shahani, Dipboye and Phillips (1990) that little is known so far about the relation of naturally occurring time management with the personality and performance of people, but it remains an important question for those working in the hierarchically organized systems. The finding that the personality and the dispositions of managers matter in time utilization (even though to a limited extent) seems interesting. There are certain inherent contradictions that work against efficient time utilization by managers. First, the general socio-cultural milieu of the country is such that an awareness of time is not acquired during the process of socialization at home, school and college, while the time-regulated nature of modern industry values it. The time factor is often involved in the punch-in and punch-out system and it continues to be seen as a flexible and stretchy factor, contingent on work/personal, organizational and social needs. Else the technology so demands. Secondly, the time factor is used more as a general defining characteristic of the job than as one specific to position/responsibilities and performance behaviour.

Managers as individuals tend to structure their time in relation to their personal goals and purposes, and their ability to make adjustments to the norms of working groups. If a majority practice time in the same manner, one's own identity remains camouflaged within the group. The inefficient use of time does not cause any cognitive dissonance and feelings of personal guilt. On the other hand, in the given socio-organizational reality, those spending time at work more efficiently suffer from multiple conflicts at the individual and social levels. They find themselves under pressure to become compatible with others who are their referents for social comparison as they are in similar positions (contributing less and getting equal or more rewards). Otherwise they practise efficient time utilization as individuals without expecting/getting any appreciation for it, and feel demoralized in the absence of any multiplier effect of their actions.

Strategy-Making, Environment and Structure

Some significant relations are observed between variables of time management and strategy-making, environment, and structure. The strategy of futurity is related to more aspects of time management in various groups whereas the proactivity strategy is related to the least. Futurity correlates positively with the time spent on work, on taking inspection rounds, on sorting out matters with ministry officials, and on unspecified activities in the public sector; on taking rounds in the profit-making group; on unspecified activities in the loss-making group; and on work, taking rounds and unspecified activities among the externality-oriented managers. It is negatively associated with time on personal care in the public sector; on discussions with juniors and peers in the private sector; on personal care in the loss-making enterprises; and on paperwork among internality-oriented managers. The correlation coefficients range between -0.31 to 0.27, and are significant in most cases.

The proactivity strategy is associated positively with the time spent on meetings by private sector managers, and with the work overload in loss-making enterprises. It is negatively associated with the time spent on personal care and on work by externality-oriented managers. It appears that activity-oriented managers spend more of their time on crucial work activities and less on those limited to personal likings and wasteful activities. They are also in all probability more intensely involved in their participation. The correlation coefficients range between 0.27 to 0.33, and are significant.

Those who use the risk-taking strategy try to communicate more with their superiors, and less with their peers and juniors, irrespective of their personal orientation. This has been more so in the public sector and in the loss-making corporations. The use of the risk-taking strategy correlates positively with the time spent by managers on discussions with their superiors in the private sector, loss-making corporations, and among internality-oriented managers; with time spent on social activities and taking rounds by internality-oriented managers; and with time spent on meetings by externality-oriented managers. It is negatively associated with the time spent on discussions with juniors and peers in the public sector, profit-making corporations and internality-oriented groups.

The strategy of innovation correlates positively with the time spent on the family and on personal care in profit-making enterprises; and on hobbies and social activities in loss-making enterprises. In profit-making enterprises, managers who spend more time on caring about themselves and their families used innovative strategies, while in the loss-making group such managers spend more time in doing things of their own interests and in socializing. It is negatively associated with the time spent on personal care in the private sector, and on hobbies by externality-oriented managers.

Managers who find the environment to be dynamic and having variety and challenge believe in the utility of frequent visits to factories and offices. The aspect of dynamism of the environment is associated positively with the time spent on taking inspection rounds in the public sector, in profit-making corporations and among externality-oriented managers. It is associated negatively with the time spent on unspecified activities in profit-making corporations; with the time spent on paperwork and meetings in the loss-making corporations; and with the time spent on meetings in internality-oriented groups. Heterogeneity in the environment is found significantly related with the time spent on discussions with superiors, meetings and taking inspection rounds in the public sector; with work overload in the private sector; with discussions with superiors, meetings, taking rounds, knowing market trends and unspecified activities in the profit-making enterprises; with time spent on social activities in the loss-making enterprises; with time spent on discussions with superiors and paperwork by the internality- oriented managers; and with time spent on meetings by the externality-oriented managers. Technologists and scientists in the private sector prefer to spend time on acquiring knowledge of market trends, while technocrats in the public sector spend more time in meetings and paperwork.

The scanning aspect of structure is associated significantly but negatively with the time spent on hobbies and paperwork in the profit-making group. It is associated negatively with the time spent on hobbies and positively with the time spent on discussions with superiors in the internality-oriented managers. The internality-oriented managers who have open communication with superiors use the scanning structure much more frequently. The technocratization aspect of structure correlates significantly and positively with the time spent on meetings in the public sector, knowing about market trends in the private sector; and miscellaneous activities in the loss-making group. It is negatively associated with the time spent on paperwork and meetings by internality-oriented managers; and positively with the time spent on paperwork in the externality-oriented managers. The differentiation aspect of structure relates negatively with the time spent on hobbies and on discussions with superiors in the public sector. It is associated positively with the time spent on work and taking rounds in the public sector; with the time spent in sorting out matters with ministry officials in the profit-making enterprises; with the time spent on social activities and taking rounds in the loss-making enterprises; with the time spent on family affairs by internality-oriented managers and with the time spent on hobbies and taking round by the externality-oriented managers. It correlates negatively with the time spent on work in loss-making corporations and by internality-oriented managers. Those who have the ability to deal actively with dynamic environments and can cope with government controls attempt diversification by overlooking procedures.

Inferences and Directions

The finding of nominal differences in time management on the basis of sector, profitability and personal orientation of managers seems to be an indicator for redesigning organizational processes and practices. Under ideal conditions when corporations have differences in terms of structure, control, organizational culture and in the choice of addressing policies, managers may be persuaded by perceived challenges to follow time efficient techniques. In reality, most corporate managers who have been recruited have similar educational qualifications and professional preparation, and are forced to operate under tight controls and restrictive policies. There is little need and inadequate pressure to use time constructively and in different ways. Irrespective of the type of industry, the time spent on major activities is regulated in an identical manner. This is similar to the observation by Knasel, Super and Kidd (1981) that the time spent on work continues to be perceived as a constraint on the freedom to manage it in a flexible manner.

Managers in both private and public sectors spend more or less the statutorily required time on work. They also spend a similar amount of time on family affairs. In all the groups the time spans spent on work, on family and on hobbies form a cluster. The time spent on work is found positively associated with the time spent on family and hobbies in both public and private sectors; in the profit-making and in the loss-making corporations; for the inter-nality-oriented and for the externality-oriented managers (the coefficients of correlations range between 0.14 and 0.40). Evans and Bartolome (1986) and Knowles and Taylor (1990) have argued that non-work activities complement, compensate for, or compete with work activities, and that work, family and leisure activities characterized the effective managers' cognitive map. It has been observed here that in the Indian social context, managers value the family for the emotional support it offers, and for the qualitatively different kinds of personal relationships one can develop within its domain of activities. It happens to be used more frequently when work is stressful. There is thus no trade-off in the time spent on work and the time spent on the family or between the time spent on work and the time spent on leisure. Whatever the managers have been doing has been consciously determined and judiciously implemented.

Senior managers thus reflect a balanced cognition. This finding is different from that of Sinha (1988) who has stated that if managers spend more time on the job, they would compulsively spend less time with the families.

In the public sector, inefficient time utilization has been seen as an inbuilt structural constraint. It has employment generation as one of its objectives, irrespective of the needs and growth of the industry. It results in overmanning at all levels, while at the same time it leaves a good number of available man-hours unutilized. There is diffusion of responsibility and an inclination to overindulge in wasteful and unproductive activities. People find it possible and easy to hide themselves behind the rules and procedures. On the one hand, managers are more often than not unable to get the work done, even if it means assigning only a small job to a person, and at the same time so many employees are without adequate work and are seen idle and indulging in gossiping. The general attitude has been to look at individual effort as dispensable as someone could always do that work (Kerr and Brunn, 1983). This is also know as the 'sucker' effect'. The variety and challenges in the environment are not attractive enough to test the utility of new structures and strategies. Several strategies seem to be relevant and can be adopted to contain the ill-effects of overmanning, if managers and bosses are serious about improvement. The strategies which seem applicable to the Indian context include the identifiability of individual performance (Kerr and Brunn, 1981); the making of anticipated evaluations of performance (Harkins and Jackson, 1985); the introduction of competition (Kravitz and Waller, 1980); devising difficult, challenging, and intrinsically interesting tasks (Harkins and Petty, 1982) and clearcut goal-setting exercises (Schnake, 1991).

Overall, the patterns of time management and time distribution are differentiative of private versus public, profit-making versus loss-making and internality-oriented versus externality-oriented managers. It appears true that time management is a multidimensional behaviour and that the dynamics of time management is quite complex (Macan et al., 1990). An obvious implication of this seems to be that if time efficient techniques have to be used, corporations would have to be restructured, and more functional procedures would have to be adopted. There has to be some congruence between the perceptions of the environment, the use of strategy-making and the type of structure, and time management techniques. To match the number of employees, the work has to be expanded so that the available hands can be gainfully utilized. The objective of employment generation may be re-examined in the light of organizational needs and resources, and the socio-cultural milieu. Further, time consciousness has to be generated at all levels through various attitudinal interventions. The focus of organizational socialization should shift from a mere talk about the use of effective time management to learning about the need, the value and the techniques of effective time utilization and putting these into practice.

5

GOAL ACHIEVEMENT

Goals for Managers

If all organized activity at the individual, unit and corporate levels
was persistent and purposeful, the achievement of predetermined
goals would be a logical indicator of managerial effectiveness. Conversely, the discrepancy between predetermined and achieved goals
would indicate either overachievement or underachievement.
Managers attempt to achieve a variety of organizational and individual
goals at work. They do so simultaneously as well as successively.
Organizational goals reflect the internal commitment of an organization to strive in predetermined directions. The goals of individual
managers reflect what they consider important, as well as possible
for them to achieve by undertaking a variety of job-related activities.
Operational organizational goals encompass the majority of the
aspects of the organization's structures and functioning. The achievement of organizational goals is thus important for justifying its raison
d'être. The clearly operationalized individual goals encompass the
managers' cognitive and affective needs, resources and constraints
that determine interactively their efficiency. Individual goals may
range from the simple need of meeting one's basic requirements,
like the economic support for oneself, to complex needs of high
standards of achievement and control over one's environment. In
general, the achievement of organizational goals encompasses the

achievement of personal goals and is accorded a high priority (Madison, Allen, Porter, Renwick and Mays, 1983).

The setting of goals has been considered an obvious need for organizations and individual managers alike. Clearly defined organizational goals offer an unambiguous basis for organizational decision-making, as these provide direct standards for individual and collective effectiveness (Locke, 1968; Mott, 1972; Price, 1972). The use of goals as a standard has been found problematic. It has been found difficult to operationalize goal achievement, particularly in organizations where goals are multiple, transitional, intangible or part of a means–end chain (Warner, 1967).

It has been observed by Perrow (1972) that if individuals are expected to choose goals from competing values and contribute to goal achievement, they must clearly understand what the goals are. The target goals reflect the desired state of affairs, while the achieved goals reflect the actual position. Latham and Locke (1979) and Locke and Latham (1990) have stated that, in whatever manner it is done, the setting of goals leads to positive behaviours, such as increased production and reduced absenteeism and injuries. The setting of goals thus seems inevitable and desirable.

The ardent supporters of the goal theory have in fact been consistent in their logic and evidence that the setting of goals works as a motivational technique in achieving targets. If the goals are highly challenging, they are better than less challenging and moderate goals, and the latter are better than having no goals. Not having any goals would mean the lack or denial of purposive and directional activities in organizations. High performance in relation to any goal should lead to higher satisfaction as people like succeeding better than failing (Locke and Latham, 1990). The choice of goals is an integration of what one desires and what one believes is possible. Also, if managers set goals that are unfair, arbitrary, and unattainable, the resulting poor performance would be unavoidable. If they set difficult goals without adequate quality control, the enterprise may be able to meet the quantitative targets at the cost of quality. If managers exert undue pressure on their juniors to get immediate results without regard to the processes and strategies, this may trigger the use of expedient and ultimately costly methods in achieving the targets. This would happen because the goals would not be accepted as standards for the evaluation of one's self and one's performance (Bandura, 1988).

Only a few Indian researchers have focused on organizational goals, in spite of the overwhelming importance of these in improving the understanding of structures, processes and practices of organizations. Of the three researches that have been found relevant, one has focused on the need for managers to disseminate information about the set organizational goals to different levels, if they are keen on effectiveness (Orpen, 1978). The issue of a link between the perceived specificity of organizational objectives and indicators of effectiveness has been examined by Mishra (1982), while Khandwalla and Jain (1984) have tried to assess the differential impact of organizational goals on job satisfaction. These two studies are however based on lower management cadres, while the goals of senior and top managers are in focus here.

Goal Achievement—Concept and Measure

It seems probable that goal achievement can be conceptualized in many ways and thus assessed differently. Goal achievement can be conceptualized as the achievement of targets set for managers as individuals or/and targets of organizations as reflected in their achievements. These can be measured by employing either subjective or/and objective indicators. This issue was addressed initially as overall effectiveness and measured by asking the senior managers /heads of the units one question: How effective have you been in your corporation in the last three years in achieving your predetermined goals? Five Likert-type response categories, ranging from 'very effective' to 'least effective' were used for obtaining responses. In the pre- tryout stage most respondents found the question somewhat vague and global. They suggested that if goal achievement has to be realistically measured, the question should be made more specific.

The detailed discussions with several managers and experts suggested the need to combine in the measure the desired as well as the achieved goals, and to make the measure more specific. Thus, in the final test, managers were first asked to indicate on a seven-point scale (range between 'below 20%' to '80% and above') where they would place the goals which they had set for themselves in their corporate capacity during the last three years or so at the beginning of the year, plan/ project etc. Having done that they were asked to place their achieved goals (what they had actually achieved during the year/plan/project) on the same seven-point scale. The achieved targets response was then subtracted from the set targets in order to find the net goal achievement. This technique has a subjective as well as an objective assessment component. It is subjective in the sense that it asks managers to provide self-ratings of their goal achievement. At the same time it is objective since it makes them pinpoint their position on a predetermined scale as to what their targets were and what they were able to achieve. The Cronbach Alpha for the measure of net goals was 0.78.

Managers' Goal Charts

The managers' responses to the question of goal achievement in terms of the goals set as well as the goals achieved over an average period of three years were interesting and consistent with the plan of assessment. They responded to the question of specific choice in the given response format quite easily. It has been observed that both in the public and private sectors managers tend to set their targets above the level of 70 per cent and achieve a level between 60-70 per cent. The mean target goals for the public sector are about 0.10 higher than those for the private sector, while the mean achieved goals are approximately 0.45 higher in the public sector. The public sector managers indicate that they are able to achieve the corporate goals once set at a significantly higher level than the private sector managers (M=3.80, SD=0.85, M=3.28, SD=1.33, t=3.47, p<0.01). This seems to belie the common observation that the public sector performs by and large much below the level of the private sector.

There has been very little variation between the profit-and loss-making corporations in terms of the targets set, as both are governed by similar policy instruments and administrative mechanisms. The achieved goals are, however, on an average (0.22), higher in the profit-making than in the loss-making corporations, and the differences are significant above the 10 per cent level. The mean net goal achievement has also been in favour of the profit-making corporations and is significant above the 10 per cent level (M=3.69, SD=0.83; M=3.38, SD=0.86, t=1.84). The expectation of significant variations by the internality-externality orientation of managers has not been supported statistically, although it indicates that the internals tend to set their targets somewhat higher than the externals and also have higher achievements (M=3.88, SD=0.84; M=3.74, SD=0.85).

Time Management

Goal achievement is found to have a positive association with the time spent by managers on work in the public sector, and equally well in the profit-and loss-making corporations and the internality and externality-oriented groups as the correlations range between r=0.11 and r=0.24, and some are statistically significant. Goal achievement correlates significantly with the time spent on family obligations and socializing in the loss- making and externality-oriented groups, and with the time spent on hobbiés, and sleeping and personal care in the private sector (the correlations range between r=0.14 and r=0.52). It appears that managers in the public sector in general, and particularly in the profit-making and internality-oriented groups are convinced that the time spent on work matters in achieving the present targets. They achieve their goals by observing the statutorily prescribed time at work and by following the time schedules to a considerable extent. The loss-making and externality-oriented groups also find time spent on work meaningful despite the performance deficits, but they use their family and social network to compensate and complement their feelings of inadequacy. The diverse and carefully monitored interests of managers of the private sector take them to various clubs and associations which serve two purposes. First, this enlarges the range of their social contacts that may eventually prove useful in their goal achievement. Second, this reduces their job induced tensions and freshens their approach to work. Planning and managing as work activities have been found relevant and given due attention by managers in the private sector, profit-making and internality-oriented groups (the correlations range between r=0.10 and r=0.46). Managers in the public sector and those who are internality-oriented take rounds of offices and factories much more regularly. Work overload has a positive association with goal achievement in all the groups (the correlations range between r=0.10 and r=0.46), indicating that the tendency to extend work to the home is a common habit of all managers at that level. In the private sector, the discussions with superiors are important (as shown by a positive and significant correlation) as these often involve the owners. They are more important than spending time on knowing about markets and unscheduled activities (correlations are negative and insignificant). Managers in all groups in the public sector spend time in knowing about markets. The externality-oriented managers spend a significant amount of time on paperwork and the internality-oriented managers spend time on residual activities (as both correlations are positive and significant).

The aspects of time management in different areas of life have explained different degrees of variance in goal achievement for various groups of managers, ranging between two and 13 per cent. Although the highest degree of variance has been explained in the goal achievement of the managers in the private sector, in no group has it been adequately meaningful. The highest negative regression weight is for the time given to hobbies, suggesting that the practice of taking some time out of the work schedule perhaps helps in reducing the discomfort arising out of the pressures of goal achievement. The time given to hobbies, social life and work is found satisfying by managers in the profit-making corporations and by those having external orientation. The time variables operate in an inverse manner in the loss-making corporations. This violates the hypothesis that effective time management automatically leads to high goal achievement.

The distribution of time on various work-related activities explains the variance in the domain of goal achievement. It is 20 per cent for the private sector, 5 per cent for the public sector, 11 per cent for profit-making organizations, 4 per cent for loss-making organizations, 9 per cent for internality-oriented managers and 10 per cent for externality-oriented managers. In all the cases, the prediction by time allocated to various work activities has been better than the time managed in different life areas, indicating that most often the primary goals of managers are synonymous with the corporate goals. The work time is thus important. The work activities which are meaningful for goal achievement are: taking rounds of workplaces in all groups; planning and managing for the public sector, profit-making and internality-oriented and externality-oriented groups; sorting out matters with ministry officials for profit-making and internality-oriented groups; discussions with superiors in the private sector, and with juniors and peers in the loss-making groups. It appears that the practice of managers' making their presence felt to juniors works to a certain extent as a motivational strategy to achieve the set goals. The time spent on planning and managing is helpful in large, complex organizations in the public sector, where diversity of structures and heterogeneity in environment are inevitable aspects of the job one has to cope with. The frequency of work taken home is common to all managers, but more so to the private sector and loss-making groups. It is used differently by managers in the private and public sectors.

Personal Orientation, Strategy-Making, Perceptions of Environment and Structure

The personal orientation of managers in the private sector correlates negatively with goal achievement, indicating that the internality-oriented managers achieve significantly higher goals, while the relationship in the public sector has been only nominal. The association for the managers in profit-making corporations is positive, indicating that the externals can manage to achieve their targets. The managers of loss-making corporations, however, need much more inner strength to achieve their goals, as the correlation for them is negative.

The positive associations of goal achievement with role perceptions, confidence, and professional commitment in all the groups are important and suggest that the achievement of set goals is facilitated by the presence of these characteristics among effective managers. These operate as the sufficient conditions for goal achievements. The use of the futurity strategy facilitates goal achievement in all groups, except in the loss-making group where managers do not score very high on futurity-orientation and have difficulties in meeting their current targets. Goal achievement of managers in the private sector correlates positively with the futurity strategy, and negatively with the variables of dynamism and heterogeneity in the environment, and differentiation aspect of structure, although the correlations are not significant (Table 5.1). Apparently, goal achievement requires a good deal of futurity-orientation among managers, but the environmental turbulence (both constant change and variety) and the need to evolve diversified structures to cope with the demands can often act as deterrents.

Goal achievement of managers in the public sector correlates positively with proactivity and futurity strategies, and the differentiation aspect of structure. In the profit-making corporations also it correlates positively with proactivity and futurity strategies. Goal achievement has low positive correlations with the technocratization and differentiation aspects of structure, indicating that the presence of technocrats and the adding of new divisions in these organizations make little difference to achievements. A ceiling effect has perhaps been reached by them.

Table 5.1: Correlations of Goal Achievement with Role Perceptions, Confidence, Professional Commitment, Strategy, Environment and Structure

Variables		PM	LM	Pr	Pu	I	E
RP		0.35**	0.34**	0.42**	0.35**	0.39**	0.32**
C		0.36**	0.41**	0.31*	0.39**	0.40**	0.38**
PC		0.21*	0.34**	0.33*	0.28**	0.37**	0.20*
I		0.01	-0.01	-0.04	-0.01	0.06	-0.15
RT	Strategy	-0.10	-0.05	0.23	-0.10	0.15	-0.22**
PA		0.30**	0.15	0.27	0.09	0.19*	0.17*
F		0.27**	-0.17*	0.22	0.16*	0.16*	0.16*
D	Environment	0.01	-0.09	-0.23	0.05	-0.16*	0.03
H		0.02	-0.06	-0.14	-0.03	0.03	-0.08
S		0.06	0.05	-0.04	0.06	0.02	0.08
T	Structure	0.06	-0.10	0.01	0.02	0.05	0.00
Di		0.12	0.17*	-0.21	0.09	-0.13	0.05

* $p < 0.05$
** $p < 0.01$

RP=Role perceptions; C=Confidence; PC=Professional commitment; I=Innovation; RT=Risk taking; PA=Proactivity; F=Futurity; D=Dynamism; H=Heterogeneity; S=Scanning; T=Technocratization; Di=Differentiation; PM=Profit-Making group; LM=Loss-Making group; Pr=Private Sector; Pu=Public Sector; I=Internals; E=Externals.

Managers in the loss-making corporations emphasize the need to use the proactivity strategy and diversified structures to overcome their present problems, but they have lower futurity-orientation, as seen by the negative association with futurity. They do attempt to be more active, and advocate the need to be assertive to make up the losses and avert crisis situations, but it has not been so in the public sector in general. The public sector managers have a work ethos in which one is encouraged to do the minimum, and do it only when asked to do so specifically rather than at one's own initiative. The internality-oriented managers use innovation and futurity strategies, and differentiated structures. They have little difficulty in coping with dynamic environments and in achieving the targets, although most contingencies in the environment are externally controlled. This is visible in the negative correlation with dynamism in the environment. The goal achievement of externality-oriented managers is facilitated positively by the use of proactivity and futurity strategies (as seen by positive correlations), and hindered by innovation and risk-taking strategies. Managers in all the groups prefer to use futurity and proactivity strategies much more frequently, and attempt diversification of structures. The use of innovation and risk-taking strategies has been found related to their personal orientation. The internality-oriented managers find the innovation strategy helpful in goal achievement, but the externality-oriented managers find that innovation and risk-taking strategies impede the achievement of set targets, as these divert attention and threaten the corporations with losses.

Managers of the private sector find the business environment turbulent and filled with a variety of uncertainties. This makes their meeting of targets difficult. Managers of the public sector really do not react to the environment negatively as they function in a highly protracted environment, devoid of any competition. Proactivity and risk-taking strategies and heterogeneity in the environment have negative values for the internality-oriented managers, while dynamism in the environment and differentiation aspects of structure have positive values. The contribution of the proactivity strategy has been significant. The aspects of structure are not found significantly associated with goal achievement in most groups, except the loss-making group which looks towards diversification of products and processes to bring a turnaround in its growth and profits. This has been so even in the internality-oriented group, but not to a significant extent.

The variables of strategy, environment and structure can predict goal achievement to the maximum of 18 per cent in the private sector, 4 per cent in the public sector, 6 per cent in the profit-making group, 8 per cent in the loss-making group, 9 per cent in the internality-oriented managers and 6 per cent in the externality-oriented managers. The addition of the internality-externality score to the regression equations containing variables of strategy, environment and structure has explained variance in goal achievement to the extent of 24 per cent in the private sector, 5 per cent in the public sector, 11 per cent in the profit-making group and 9 per cent in the loss-making group. Thus, in the private sector and in profit-making corporations, the personal orientation of managers matters more than others.

Composite Trends

The selected predictors of time management, time allocated to work activities, strategy-making, environment, structure and the personal orientation of managers in different groups are helpful in explaining the optimum variance of 24 per cent in the private sector (Table 5.2), 10 per cent in the public sector (Table 5.3), 21 per cent in the profit-making units and 10 per cent in the loss-making units (Tables 5.4 and 5.5) and 12 per cent each in the internality and externality-oriented managers (Tables 5.6 and 5.7).

In the case of the private sector, the maximum variance has been explained by the variables of strategy, environment, structure and internality-externality of managers. Proactivity and risk-taking strategies, and heterogeneity in the environment make positive contributions to the goal achievement of managers in the private sector. A higher technocratization seems to affect goal achievement adversely. It appears that technocrats use a rational method of analysis, and this may not always prove productive. The achievement of goals also requires a passionate commitment on the part of managers. The positively contributing variables in the loss-making corporations

Table 5.2: Regression Analysis for Private Sector Managers.
Dependent Variable: Goal Achievement

Predictors	Df	B	T	R	R^2	P
Proactivity	9,36	0.87	2.47	0.49	0.24	0.05
Heterogeneity	9,36	0.34	0.92	–	–	ns
Internality–Externality	9,36	0.22	1.69	–	–	ns
Risk-taking	9,36	0.18	1.28	–	–	ns
Innovation	9,36	-0.14	1.17	–	–	ns
Technocratization	9,36	-0.11	0.74	–	–	ns
Scanning	9,36	-0.08	0.93	–	–	ns
Futurity	9,36	-0.03	0.53	–	–	ns
Dynamism	9,36	-0.02	0.31	–	–	ns
Differentiation	9,36	-0.01	0.08	–	–	ns

Df=Degree of Freedom; B=Standardized regression weights; T=T ratio; R=Multiple Correlation R; P=Level of Significance

Table 5.3: Regression Analysis for Public Sector Corporations.
Dependent Variable: Goal Achievement

Predictors	Df	B	T	R	R^2	P
Planning and managing	9,258	0.74	2.19	0.32	0.10	0.05
Rounds	9,258	0.62	2.56	–	–	0.05
Proactivity	9,258	-0.51	2.07	–	–	0.05
Risk-taking	9,258	-0.51	2.19	–	–	0.05
Social life	9,258	0.30	1.49	–	–	ns
Internality–Externality	9,258	-0.10	1.37	–	–	ns
Paperwork	9,258	-0.09	1.06	–	–	ns
Work overload	9,258	-0.06	0.86	–	–	ns
Innovation	9,258	-0.01	0.24	–	–	ns
Sleeping and personal care	9,258	-0.01	0.19	–	–	ns

Df=Degree of Freedom; B=Standardized regression weights; T=T ratio; R=Multiple Correlation R; P=Level of Significance

Table 5.4: Regression Analysis for Profit-Making Corporations.
Dependent Variable: Goal Achievement

Predictors	Df	B	T	R	R^2	P
Rounds	8,138	0.97	2.95	0.46	0.21	0.01
Internality–Externality	8,138	0.84	2.72	–	–	0.01
Proactivity	8,138	-0.68	2.29	–	–	0.05
Work overload	8,138	0.57	2.05	–	–	0.05
Planning and managing	8,138	0.41	1.99	–	–	0.10
Social life	8,138	0.40	1.83	–	–	0.10
Risk-taking	8,138	-0.37	1.89	–	–	0.10
Paperwork	8,138	-0.03	0.63	–	–	ns
Sleeping and personal care	8,138	-0.02	0.34	–	–	ns

Df=Degree of Freedom; B=Standardized regression weights; T=T ratio; R=Multiple Correlation R; P=Level of Significance

Table 5.5: Regression Analysis for Loss-Making Corporations.
Dependent Variable: Goal Achievement

Predictors	Df	B	T	R	R^2	P
Futurity	9,111	0.66	2.12	0.31	0.10	0.05
Differentiation	9,111	0.62	1.98	–	–	0.10
Internality–Externality	9,111	0.44	1.16	–	–	ns
Technocratization	9,111	0.35	1.06	–	–	ns
Scanning	9,111	0.31	0.35	–	–	ns
Risk-taking	9,111	0.30	0.57	–	–	ns
Dynamism	9,111	0.08	0.33	–	–	ns
Innovation	9,111	0.04	0.40	–	–	ns
Proactivity	9,111	0.02	0.29	–	–	ns
Heterogeneity	9,111	-0.01	0.02	–	–	ns

Df=Degree of Freedom; B=Standardized regression weights; T=T ratio; R=Multiple Correlation R; P=Level of Significance

Table 5.6: Regression Analysis for Internality-Oriented Managers.
Dependent Variable: Goal Achievement

Predictors	Df	B	T	R	R^2	P
Rounds	8,119	1.00	2.45	0.35	0.12	0.01
Proactivity	8,119	-0.48	1.96	–	–	0.10
Planning and managing	8,119	0.42	1.79	–	–	0.10
Risk-taking	8,119	0.26	1.48	–	–	ns
Social life	8,119	0.20	0.43	–	–	ns
Paperwork	8,119	0.08	0.43	–	–	ns
Sleeping and personal care	8,119	0.07	0.22	–	–	ns
Dynamism	8,119	0.07	0.94	–	–	ns
Work overload	8,119	-0.05	0.21	–	–	ns

Df=Degree of Freedom; B=Standardized regression weights; T=T Ratio; R=Multiple Correlation; P=Level of Significance

Table 5.7: *Regression Analysis for Externality-Oriented Managers.*
Dependent Variable: Goal Achievement

Predictors	Df	B	T	R	R^2	P
Paperwork	7,132	0.47	1.89	0.35	0.12	0.10
Social life	7,132	0.41	1.75	–	–	0.10
Risk-taking	7,132	0.34	1.19	–	–	ns
Rounds	7,132	0.26	1.21	–	–	ns
Planning and managing	7,132	0.19	1.35	–	–	ns
Proactivity	7,132	0.08	0.79	–	–	ns
Work overload	7,132	-0.07	0.73	–	–	ns
Sleeping and personal care	7,132	-0.03	0.50	–	–	ns

Df=Degree of Freedom; B=Standardized regression weights; T=T ratio; R=Multiple Correlation R; P=Level of Significance

are differentiation and scanning aspects of structure, and dynamism in the environment, indicating that the structural and environmental variables along with futurity are meaningful in goal achievement.

The time spent on social life contributed positively to the goal achievement of managers in the profit-making group and in internality- and externality-oriented managers; to time on planning and managing in the public sector and the internality- and externality-oriented groups; and time on taking rounds of workplaces in the public sector, and in profit-making and externality-oriented groups. Risk-taking and proactivity strategies have made positive contributions to goal achievement in the private sector. These, however, operate negatively in the public sector, and in profit-making and internality-oriented groups. Dynamism in the environment has a low positive value in the loss-making corporations and for internals, while heterogeneity has a positive value only in the private sector. In the profit-making corporations, the strategy of actively engaging in task accomplishment and taking risks are negatively valued. The internality score contributes to the variance in goal achievement of managers in the public sector and within this sector in profit-making corporations. The differentiation aspect of structure is seen as a much more positive mechanism by the loss-making group. Paperwork proves to be a valued activity for externality-oriented managers.

Senior managers constitute the significant others for all employees.

The norms of the corporation and the quality of leadership that managers can give should be relevant in encouraging the setting of high standards (Peters and Waterman, 1982). In fact, goal achievement has not been highly predicted by the chosen predictors in any group, although a few variables are meaningful. This may be seen as a critical reflection on the quality of leadership in reality. This finding is different from other researchers who have found high performing managers to be goal directed, with a capacity to realistically size up the performance possibilities in a given situation, and to communicate a sense of direction. In a study of 90 leaders from different walks of life, Bennis and Nanus (1985) have observed that the management of attention through vision is the creation of focus. This 'pulls' people towards managers, and gives them a sense of accomplishment. The competitive performance management begins with the organizational system for establishing performance objectives, namely the strategic and business planning cycle (Evans, 1986). It appears from the observations in this study that the socio-political and economic environments act in a highly resistant manner, and constrain the organizational setting of goal achievement. The manager's vision is delimited and so are the achievements.

Emergent Issues

The findings highlight certain interesting issues for researchers, practising managers and policymakers. For example, if the goals are set externally for the organizations, (by ministries in the case of the public sector and owners in the case of the private sector) managers can only try to manipulate the organizational contingencies with limited success. Such determined goals may not necessarily be the pragmatic and achievable goals, but only the broad guidelines. Managers may try to achieve, but may/may not succeed. Even if they do achieve, it may not be what they feel committed to. The situation thus seems to be quite complex. Managers in the private sector spend more time in meeting their superiors. They have a higher urge to achieve their personal goals. A similar observation has been reported by Porter, Allen and Angle (1981).

Structurally, the private sector has relatively less complex organizations, and the setting of higher targets has perhaps some meaning for managers as they can be directly pressurized to achieve them.

They also have access to close monitoring. In the public sector, however, the links among the multilevel setting of goals, managerial efforts, available resources and group achievements are often determined on a social and temporal basis. Most managers may not see the set goals as challenging enough to make a real effort. They then fail to motivate the juniors in the absence of any reward-giving power at their disposal, and their inability to provide timely feedback. They often feel satisfied in setting moderate-level, safe and convenient goals. Those who succeed in achieving the set goals tend to indulge in self- appreciation without looking at the global reality, and those who fail tend to get demoralized and are unhappy. These findings are in line with some other researches. Mento, Locke and Klein (1992) have noted in their experiments that high goals are more instrumental than low goals with respect to both immediate and internal benefits and remote external benefits. Many managers observe that the manner of distributing resources and the nature of the manpower recruited hinder the performance of organizations, in which merit and objectivity are constantly compromised. The problem of goal achievement lies thus in bridging the gaps between different policies backed by political motivations, and the mechanisms of implementation available to managers to achieve these goals efficiently in an inefficiency-infested culture. This discrepancy should be taken note of when managers set goals and have great expectations of achieving them. Also managers must learn to challenge employees by raising standards on an incremental basis to make set goals more acceptable and less stressful.

The setting and achievement of goals in the two sectors require that differential emphasis is placed on different personal and organizational attributes. Managers with the same skills can perform differently in different sectors. Given the same organizational constraints, some managers perform poorly, some adequately, and some put in a good performance. This indicates the importance of interactive mechanisms and mediating variables like perceived salience of goals, motivation, problem solving efforts, feedback, etc.

The variations in capability and demands should be kept in view while setting the targets. It has been observed by Krishna Kumar (1982) that in the Indian context the meeting of national priorities happens to be a salient goal for the public sector but not for the private sector. The private sector often chooses not to venture into product market areas having difficulty in securing inputs, but the public sector cannot refrain from it. The management of the private sector adheres to a more organic and paternalistic, but less technocratic and altruistic system of functioning. The public sector has a long-term planning perspective and a more elaborate budgeting system, as it has more public resources invested in its corporations. The public sector enterprises show a relatively higher degree of pioneering strategically important products and technologies, while the private sector is satisfied with higher levels of adaptability and profitability, thus making the goal emphasis different.

Goals are expected to guide and motivate performance. These should help to build people's beliefs in their capabilities. In reality, however, since the goals in both the sectors are extraneously determined, managers accept them, but do not feel internally committed to achieve them. Although goal commitment has motivational properties separate from those associated with goal setting (Naylor and Ilgen, 1984), it is necessary for achievement. Commitment should encourage persistent and increased effort. It should discourage persons from giving up the effort till they succeed. It should motivate juniors to work towards an accepted goal (McCaul, Hinsz and McCaul, 1987). It is also true that the managerial effort alone may not enhance group performance if managers have not discovered the best way to match motivational factors with employee attributes in order to accomplish tasks collectively.

6

ROLE PERCEPTIONS

Managerial Roles

Most corporate systems (private and public) in India have grown over the years in size and have become complex structures in response to changing technology, politico-economic needs, customer types and environments. These have made multiple demands on their capabilities, resources and arrangements. Management functions have expanded beyond the technical and financial areas to incorporate sales, marketing (domestic and export) and human resource development. Corporate bodies have redefined the existing roles of managers and have identified new role prescriptions at all levels, particularly so at the senior levels. While the roles at the lower levels have been specified and documented, the roles at the higher levels of organizations continue to have inherent ambiguities, despite the experience of persistent problems. This is particularly true of the public sector which has a more open system than the private sector.

A number of researchers and practitioners have attempted to specify some roles of senior and top managers as a broad framework of expectations (Hales, 1986). They differ in their perceptions of what should be the major roles of managers. Chandler (1962) has identified the importance of the role of top managers in planning, appraising and coordinating, but he has not specified and given details of the implicit processes involved in the performance of these roles. Managerial roles have often been seen as positional variables and operationalized in terms of expected functions and standards (Mintzberg, 1973). The important roles of managers have been identified as those of leader, entrepreneur, disseminator, negotiator, resource allocator, environment monitor, disturbance handler, figurehead and liaison, and spokesperson. All these roles relate to different areas of responsibility, authority, equality and identity. A confirmation of these roles has been noted by Kurke and Aldrich (1979). According to Leavitt (1975), outstanding managers exercise imaginative problem solving and implementation of plans and programmes. Horton (1986) has assigned four major roles to competent managers, namely: goal and action management, direction of others, human resource management and leadership. Further, managers may perform well in some specific roles and not in others. Roles have also been classified as decisional and informational roles (Shapira and Dunbar, 1980).

The persons who play the roles and the ways in which roles are played, have emerged in recent years as important variables affecting role performance. It is believed that some managers are by nature more self-efficacious than others, and can frequently manipulate the situational contingencies to their advantage. The degree of self-efficacy thus affects the clarity with which managers conceptualize and implement their roles.

Role Perceptions: Concept and Measure

Role perceptions are important in understanding managers' job-related attitudes. These are linked to goal achievement directly as well as indirectly (Bedeian, Armenakis and Curran, 1980). The centrality of the position of managers in the organization makes it imperative for them to perceive and understand their roles clearly, so that they can send clear messages both to their seniors and juniors. They are accountable to the seniors and have obligations towards the juniors (Lyons, 1971; Beehr and Newman, 1978). A senior manager must understand clearly what role he/she is expected to play according to the requirements laid down by the government, the chairman cum managing director, or persons at other organizational levels. Tensions and conflicts can arise because of incongruity or ambiguity at any level, and this can impair one's effectiveness. Some incongruities may be germane to managerial roles and beyond one's control, yet a knowledge of these and one's coping ability may facilitate the search and choice of alternative strategies in the organizational context.

The clarity in one's perception of the role is considered basic to the performance of the role and thus desired by individuals at all levels in the organizations. It affects individual behaviours as well as organizational outcomes in an intricate manner. Two major types of role ambiguities have been identified by Kahn, Wolfe, Quinn, Snoek and Rosenthal (1964). The first type is called task ambiguity and it results from lack of information about the proper definition of the job, its goals and permissible means of achieving them. This can manifest itself in three specific forms, namely: ambiguity regarding what is required, ambiguity about how responsibilities are to be carried out and ambiguity about the role players/setters themselves. This demands that managers as actors should have clear ideas of the scope of responsibilities, expectations, procedures and available mechanisms, and clarity of conviction and communication to meet the obligations towards others. All three types of task-specific ambiguities are inherent in most decision-making roles, and make demands on managers to use all the skills, abilities and resources at their disposal in order to provide clear interpretations for themselves and to send clear messages to others. It is believed that the more skilled, able and resourceful the managers are, the more successful they would be in managing this type of ambiguity.

The second type of role ambiguity is related to the socio-emotional aspects of one's role performance, such as the effects on one's well-being, the role set or the organization as a whole. It can affect one's functioning at the individual as well as at the collective level. At the individual level, one may experience feelings of futility and lowered self-confidence. At the corporate level, one may choose contingencies that can result in inefficiency, wastage and losses. The lack of clarity in role perceptions has been found to constrain managers' performance (Porter and Lawler, 1968), and the realization of their need for power and the need for competition (Miner, 1978).

Most behavioural scientists and practical managers believe that a productive work culture would emerge in a corporation when managers can make employees at all levels clearly understand and efficiently perform their roles. Mossholder, Bedeian and Armenakis (1981) have examined the effects of role perceptions, organizational level, and self-esteem on satisfaction and performance, and the complex interrelationships existing among these variables. Some other earlier researches have reported that role perceptions are consistently related to attitudinal outcomes (Schuler, 1975; Szilagyi, 1977). Mintzberg (1979) has argued that the differences in managerial work are related to the relative importance of managerial roles across hierarchical levels and functional specialities. The top management has to give considerable attention to external roles (e.g., liaison officer, spokesperson, figure-head) responsible for the management of interactions between the environment and the organization, while managers at lower levels tend to focus more on situations specific to work and have a short-term outlook. Pavett and Lau (1983) have hypothesized that hierarchical levels and functional specialities of managers influence their roles and the required skills, knowledge and abilities. They have found evidence to support their thesis.

At the higher level, role ambiguity and the consequent stress result from the conflicting roles one is expected to perform. Even when managers have clear perceptions of what is expected of them they may encounter unnatural and forced situations of inaction, accompanied by expressions of ambivalent feelings, because of the high stakes of responsibility placed on them and the multiple-level pressures. Abdel-Halim (1980) has observed that the attributes of the person (need for achievement, locus of control), and the situation (job scope) jointly moderate the effects of role ambiguity on affective outcomes. In comparison to persons who score high on personal and situational attributes, persons who score low on both attributes react more negatively when they perceive their roles to be ambiguous.

The available research literature has not been unanimous in suggesting that the clarity in role perceptions is positively associated with higher performance, as the issue has only been scantily examined. Researchers have also given little attention to how people occupy roles in varying degrees, or to what extent they are psychologically present during particular episodes of role performance. Individuals may differ in their role perceptions because of the likelihood of using varying degrees of themselves, physically, cognitively and emotionally, in their roles (Kahn, 1990a). This seems to be true of top-level and senior managers, though there are hardly any researches focusing on senior managers. Hamner and Tosi (1974) have observed that individuals at higher levels react more negatively to role ambiguity, implying that the higher the position in the organization, the greater should be the desired and achieved clarity in role perceptions.

It appears that, at a more mundane level, the extent of clarity that managers at the senior level have in their perceptions of their authority, their rights, responsibilities, obligations, powers of decision-making and expectations of the organizations, would indicate their ability to perform the programmed aspects of their roles, while at the planning level it would enable them to draw a line between the programmed and discretionary components of their roles. The clarity about the programmed aspects of their roles would be important, as this would be a necessary component in the performance of one's roles, and thus in getting the work done. This would also determine whether one would be able to comprehend and use the discretionary components of the roles (the sufficient component in each role).

The development of a measure of role perceptions began with a content analysis of the documents related to different expectations and actions of senior and top-level managers, and on the basis of personal discussions with them in different types of corporations. Fifteen managerial roles were culled from these discussions and a list was prepared. Items written focused on each one of them. The items covered a wide variety of role obligations ranging from job responsibilities to the recognition of juniors. The response to these items required each manager to place himself/herself in the given position in the enterprise and to rate oneself for clarity in role perceptions by using a five-point forced choice response format. The technique provided a mix of self-report and objective assessments. Subsequently, four items were deleted and eleven times were retained. This list was presented to 20 managers and their responses were examined. Since the results were found satisfactory, they were used in the final measure. The minimum possible score on the scale was 11 and the maximum score 55, the neutral score being 33. The Cronbach Alpha for the measure was 0.84.

Role Perceptions of Managers

Senior managers have varied perceptions of their roles, although irrespective of their sectoral identity, profit status and personal orientation, all the managers in the study scored significantly above the theoretical mean. The mean role perception scores for various corporations ranged between 41.92 and 49.15. Most corporate managers have a high degree of clarity about their role perceptions, approximately in the region of 60-80 per cent, but the differences are there within that range, which may be crucial to their performance by virtue of their positions. The managers having a mean score of 44 plus happened to be in modern industries like petroleum and oils, power, computer technology, engineering, consultancy, fertilizers and services. The corporate managers, who have lower mean scores, are in general in the traditional and loss-making industries like drugs and chemicals, processing, textiles, agriculture and some services. The managers in the private sector (M=47.83, SD=6.33), in profit-making corporations, (M=45.71, SD=5.86) and the internality-oriented mangers (M=46.23, SD=5.73) demonstrate higher clarity than their counterparts in the public sector (M=45.21, SD=6.01), loss-making corporations (M=44.60, SD=6.15) and externality-oriented (M=44.27, SD=6.45) groups. Therefore, to a good extent, the findings are in the expected direction.

It seems that managers in different groups derive role clarity from the same as well as from different sources. The private sector managers perceive their roles clearly, more because of their pinpointed responsibility and high accountability. The managers in the profit-making corporations do so because of the lower degree of interpersonal conflicts and tensions with the controlling ministries as well as within the organizations, the important fact remaining that they are earning profits. Their success reinforces a positive self-image of themselves, which perhaps further enhances their ability to perceive their roles clearly. The opposite is true about managers in most loss-making corporations. The internals have greater clarity about their roles because of their inner strength, confidence and ability to control the conditions of role enactment and exercise. The related personal attribute of self-esteem is a relevant moderator and acts as a variable in role performance according to some researchers (Mossholder et al., 1981).

Although the degree of role clarity has been sufficiently high among the public sector managers in this study, the findings are at variance to other researches. Singh and Paul (1985) have observed that managers in the public sector in particular have a good deal of role ambiguity. They argue that role ambiguity among public sector managers stems from their overwhelming concern for the role of others rather than their own roles. Managers, who can talk volumes about others, refuse to think clearly about their own roles and obligations. The emphasis is on what others do/not do, rather than what they do/do not do.

Time Management

The way managers use their time is considered an important dimension of variations in role perceptions. It has been observed by Macan et al. (1990) that time management is positively related to role clarity, and thus to performance. In this research, the clarity in role perceptions of managers in the private sector has been found significantly associated with the time they are able to manage for family and hobbies along with work (correlations are positive and range between 0.14 and 0.21). With regard to work, it is particularly associated with the time spent on work activities like discussions with superiors and planning and managing (correlations are positive and significant). The public sector managers having clear role perceptions manage time well only on work (as the value of r is positive), and that too on time spent on knowing about markets and with work overload. In the profit-making corporations, the time managed for work and the unscheduled activities are seen as important for clear role perceptions, as both correlations are positive and significant. In the loss-making corporations, the managers spend time (beside work) on family and hobbies. At work the time given to the activities of planning and managing, knowing the market trends and unscheduled activities are relevant to clear role perceptions (correlations range between 0.17 and 0.23). While the roles are perceived more clearly by managers in the private sector and profit-making group, the time management correlates of role perceptions are comparable for the managers in the private sector and loss-making corporations, and for the public sector and profit-making corporations. It appears that the focus of the public sector managers in general, and profit-making corporate management in particular, is on managing work roles, while those in the loss-making corporations and the private sector are pressurized to play enlarged and multiple roles to earn maximally, to avert losses and to make a turn-around in profits. Their view of time management has been more expansive as they try to spend time in a balanced manner in different areas of life and on core activities at work. This differs from the time spent in over-concern with work and acquisition of knowledge of market trends in the public sector and profit-making group.

The personal orientation of managers makes some difference in the relationship of time management with the clarity of role perceptions. The clarity in role perceptions of internality-oriented managers is significantly associated with the time given to social life and with discussions with superiors (correlations are -0.15 and -0.20). It is positively associated with planning and managing, meetings and knowing market trends (correlations average 0.16). In the case of externality-oriented managers, the role perceptions relate with time given to sleeping and personal care, discussions with superiors, juniors and peers, planning and managing, paperwork, taking rounds of the workplace, and sorting out with the ministries (correlations range between 0.22 and 0.69). The externality-oriented managers with clear role perceptions thus spend significantly more time on diverse work activities involving interpersonal relationships at many levels. On the contrary, internals cultivate interpersonal relationships, that are focused on work.

The time given to work has proved to be an important predictor of managers' role perceptions in all groups. This suggests that work remains central to the understanding of role obligations of managers in general. Although it may also be said that the work time being statutorily fixed, all managers at a given position find it possible to define the programmed component of their roles much more authentically and in a compatible manner. All managerial roles include programmed and discretionary components in their required roles. Senior managers are expected to mobilize personal resources, authority and power, and manage their time to influence the individuals and the processes of the organization they work for.

The various aspects of time management explain approximately 25 per cent of the variance in role perceptions for managers in the private sector, and 8 per cent for managers in public sector corporations. In both the sectors, the important predictors have been the time spent on sleeping and personal care and on work activities. Time management explains approximately 15 per cent of the variance in role perceptions of managers in the profit-making corporations, as against the 7 per cent variance for the loss-making corporations. The time spent on work made much higher contribution in the loss-making corporations, as against the profit-making ones. The aspects of time management predict the role perceptions of externals to be better (13 per cent) than the internals (6 per cent). The frequency of work taken home is found to make a positive contribution to clarity in the role perceptions of the public sector, and particularly in those of the loss-making and externality-oriented groups. If they invest long hours in work they do try to define their roles clearly. Additionally, for the public sector the hobbies and residual activities weigh significantly. The time spent on social life has been weighted more negatively by internals than by externals. Evidently, managers who have more inner strength find that the time spent on social life is wasteful and unproductive. Conversely, managers who are keen on identifying external reinforcements perceive the time spent on social life to be useful both at the personal as well as at organizational levels.

The time spent on various work activities account for only 9 per cent of the variance in the role perceptions of the public sector managers, 32 per cent of variance for the managers of the private sector, 12 per cent for managers in loss-making corporations, 9 per cent for managers in profit-making corporations, 13 per cent for externals, and 14 per cent for internals. The activities of planning, acquiring knowledge of market trends and meetings and the frequency of work taken home make significant contributions in the public sector, for profit- and loss-making corporations, and for internals and externals. The discussions with superiors are relevant for internals and for those in the private sector. Discussions with superiors have a negative weight in the profit-making group, implying that too much discussion with superiors does not make them gain a clearer understanding of their roles. On the other hand, they feel more confused at times. They have perhaps already reached the outer limit.

Strategy-Making, Environment and Structure

All managers with a higher degree of clarity in role perceptions tend to score positively on the futurity strategy, indicating that, in general, if the managers are clear about their roles and obligations, they would adopt futurity-oriented strategies in handling organizational affairs (Table 6.1). The prognostic view of the organization that they adopt would necessarily be for their subjective well-being at the individual level, but would also contribute to the strength of the organization as they should carry out activities in a purposeful manner.

Table 6.1: Correlations of Role Perceptions, with Goal Achievement, Confidence, Professional Commitment, Strategy, Environment and Structure

Variables		Pu	Pr	PM	LM	I	E
GA		0.35**	0.42**	0.35**	0.34**	0.39**	0.32**
C		0.69**	0.90**	0.68**	0.70**	0.68**	0.69**
PC		0.55**	0.57**	0.60**	0.50**	0.53**	0.56**
I		0.13	0.28	0.06	0.22**	0.16*	0.11
RT	Strategy	-0.11	-0.20	-0.23*	0.08	-0.05	-0.14
PA		0.12	0.17	0.12	0.12	0.15	0.11
F		0.26**	0.43**	0.27**	0.21*	0.34**	0.18*
D	Environment	0.10	-0.21	-0.02	0.22*	0.05**	0.19*
H		0.08	-0.04	0.07	0.12	0.12	0.07
S		0.06	0.27	0.01	0.13	0.02	0.05
T	Structure	0.02	-0.02	0.07	0.06	-0.06	-0.01
Di		0.17*	-0.04	0.14	0.22*	0.11	0.20*

* $p < 0.05$
** $p < 0.01$

GA=Goal ·Achievement; C=Confidence; PC=Professional commitment; I=Innovations; RT=Risk taking; PA=Proactivity; F=Futurity; D=Dynamism; H=Heterogeneity; S=Scanning; T=Technocratization; Di=Differentiation; PM=Profit-making; LM=Loss-Making; Pr=Private, Pu=Public; I=Internals; E=Externals.

There are some variations related to sector and profit status in the use of strategies. The private and public sectors, and within the latter the loss-making corporations and internality-oriented managers with clear perceptions of their roles and accepting the responsibility for themselves, adopt the innovation strategy relatively more frequently. They do so either to achieve growth or/and to secure a turnaround in performance, even if it has been forced on them by the situational contingencies. The externality-oriented managers seem to have the advantage of clear perceptions of roles, although via another route, namely, by handling the turbulent environment through the process of expanding, diversifying and managing available organizational resources efficaciously.

Managers in the private sector, perceiving their roles more clearly, use scanning mechanisms much more regularly than managers in the public sector (who use diversification), particularly in the loss-making corporations, and externality-oriented managers. The role of personality has been relevant in the role perceptions of managers in both sectors, but in different directions. The public sector managers have slightly less internality and less clarity in role perceptions than the private sector managers. In the profit-making group the scores on both variables are higher than in the loss-making group. It may thus be inferred that externality does not necessarily operate as a negative concomitant in clear role perceptions. Its effect is perhaps contingent to some extent on the profit status of a corporation.

The issue of congruence between personality dispositions and role expectations in performance, and thus effectiveness, has been considered in earlier researches (Getzels and Guba, 1955), but the findings remain at variance. What would be the degree of congruence between personality and the role implicit in any behavioural act is contingent on several factors, some of which are not even under one's personal control. Managers with different personality dispositions tend to elicit different responses from individuals working with them. For example, persuasive managers elicit more active and cooperative pressures in the working group than egoistic managers. Also, managers having different personal orientations make use of different strategies in meeting their role expectations and in achieving the organizational goals.

The finding that internality-oriented managers have clearer role perceptions than externals confirms the belief that personality matters. This observation is also supported by other researchers (Organ and Greene, 1974). Organ and Greene have reported a positive relationship between externality and role ambiguity, implying that internals would have a higher degree of clarity in perceived roles. Personality is an important correlate of role ambiguity according to Bedeian et al. (1980). Those having greater clarity about their roles are found less impulsive, more aggressive and competitive, and they demonstrate greater self-control. They are more certain about the clear outline of their self-role in the organizational context, and thus have greater promise of being effective in a wider range of situations.

In all the groups the role perceptions are positively associated with goal achievement, confidence and professional commitment (Table 6.1), implying that the greater the clarity the managers have in the perceptions of roles, the better they perform. They also display more confidence and professional commitment. It is felt that managers should use their abilities to assess the constraints imposed by the organizational environment, structure, technology, policies, procedures, and social and political relationships in order to comprehend their roles clearly and to act effectively.

Successful managers attend to interpersonal processes and the people they come into contact with. They try to understand the strengths and weaknesses of their colleagues, the relationships that are important to them, their agendas and priorities. Several researchers have observed that role perceptions are more consistently related to attitudes than behavioural outcomes (Schuler, 1975; Szilagyi et al., 1976). But in practice, attitudes are more closely related to behavioural acts. Managers who perceive their roles clearly, desire that others do so, and find ways to enhance their joint effectiveness.

It is expected that effective managers will create appropriate performance conditions by allocating people and other resources to various functions, and will continually adapt their organizational roles and practices to ongoing changes in the available resources and situational contingencies (Kotter, 1982). In all corporations, the management function is viewed as the key to unambiguous communication of messages which is desirable to increase innovations and productivity. The top-level and senior managers are expected to display role clarity and vision reflecting corporate values, and communicate these to subordinate personnel through words, symbols and actions (Kouzes and Posner, 1988). Perceiving the senior managers to be effective communicators of roles and vision, are the subordinates who are supportive and show greater commitment, higher productivity and clarity about their expectations than those not communicating with their managers. The effects of managers' actions are found to vary across different organizational settings, but they all have definite impact on employee commitment, performance, involvement, job satisfaction and role perceptions. Niehoff, Enz and Grover (1990) have reported a significant relationship of role ambiguity with vision sharing and commitment of managers.

The different aspects of strategy-making and perceptions of environment and structure explain approximately a variance of 11 per cent in role perceptions of managers in the public sector, 47 per cent in the private sector, 12 per cent in the loss-making corporations, 16 per cent in the profit-making corporations, 15 per cent for internals and 11 per cent for externals. Futurity and risk-taking strategies emerge important for all groups, except the loss-making group. Additionally, the differentiation aspect of structure is significant for managers in the public sector, in loss-and profit-making corporations and for externals. The innovation strategy and dynamism in environment are important for the private sector, loss-making corporations and internals. Evidently, all senior managers are expected to have a good futurity-orientation, have some degree of risk-taking, enact the environment as dynamic and always changing, and identify the coping roles, and they do attempt to live up to these expectations.

Composite Trends and Directions

The selected variables of time management, strategy-making, environment, structure and personal orientation explain a maximum variance of 64 per cent in role perceptions of the private sector managers (Table 6.2), 28 per cent variance in the public sector (Table 6.3), 33 per cent in the loss-making corporations (Table 6.4), 32 per cent in the profit-making corporations (Table 6.5), 32 per cent for internality-oriented (Table 6.6) and 30 per cent for externality-oriented (Table 6.7).

Tables 6.2: Regression Analysis for Private Sector Enterprises.
Dependent Variable: Role Perceptions

Predictors	Df	B	T	R	R^2	P
Innovation	13,32	1.04	2.67	0.80	0.64	0.01
Dynamism	13,32	0.86	1.89	–	–	0.10
Planning and managing	13,32	0.81	1.88	–	–	0.10
Work	13,32	0.63	1.68	–	–	0.10
Heterogeneity	13,32	0.54	1.68	–	–	0.10
Risk-taking	13,32	0.45	1.76	–	–	0.10
Futurity	13,32	0.41	1.65	–	–	ns
Differentiation	13,32	0.33	1.27	–	–	ns
Markets	13,32	0.31	0.54	–	–	ns
Internality–Externality	13,32	-0.21	0.54	–	–	ns
Proactivity	13,32	-0.10	0.15	–	–	ns
Social life	13,32	-0.11	0.10	–	–	ns
Technocratization	13,32	0.04	0.06	–	–	ns
Work overload	13,32	-0.02	0.02	–	–	ns

Df=Degree of Freedom; B=Standardized regression weights; T=T Ratio; R=Multiple Correlation; P=Level of Significance.

Table 6.3: Regression Analysis for Public Sector Corporations.
Dependent Variable: Role Perceptions

Predictors	Df	B	T	R	R^2	P
Planning and managing	13,254	0.96	2.33	0.53	0.28	0.01
Futurity	13,254	0.75	2.06	–	–	0.05
Differentiation	13,254	0.54	2.03	–	–	0.05
Risk-taking	13,254	0.50	1.77	–	–	0.10
Work overload	13,254	0.48	1.75	–	–	0.10
Internality–Externality	13,254	0.35	1.69	–	–	0.10
Innovation	13,254	0.25	1.66	–	–	0.10
Scanning	13,254	-0.16	1.47	–	–	ns
Markets	13,254	-0.36	1.46	–	–	ns
Social life	13,254	-0.57	1.27	–	–	ns
Heterogeneity	13,254	0.17	1.44	–	–	ns
Work	13,254	-0.10	0.38	–	–	ns
Proactivity	13,254	-0.05	0.23	–	–	ns
Technocratization	13,254	-0.01	0.07	–	–	ns

Df=Degree of Freedom; B=Standardized regression weights; T=T Ratio; R=Multiple Correlation; P=Level of Significance.

Table 6.4: Regression Analysis for Loss-Making Corporations.
Dependent Variable: Role Perceptions

Predictors	Df	B	T	R	R^2	P
Differentiation	12,108	0.72	2.31	0.58	0.33	0.05
Planning and managing	12,108	0.70	2.12	–	–	0.05
Dynamism	12,108	0.29	1.89	–	–	0.10
Social life	12,108	0.23	1.81	–	–	0.10
Innovation	12,108	0.17	1.55	–	–	ns
Work overload	12,108	-0.27	1.71	–	–	ns
Proactivity	12,108	-0.17	1.16	–	–	ns
Futurity	12,108	-0.46	1.19	–	–	ns
Scanning	12,108	0.11	0.88	–	–	ns
Heterogeneity	12,108	-0.15	0.87	–	–	ns
Work overload	12,108	0.12	0.76	–	–	ns
Internality–Externality	12,108	0.07	0.57	–	–	ns
Technocratization	12,108	-0.03	0.57	–	–	ns

Df=Degree of Freedom; B=Standardized regression weights; T=T Ratio; R=Multiple Correlation; P=Level of Significance.

Table 6.5: Regression Analysis for Profit-Making Corporations.
Dependent Variable: Role Perceptions

Predictors	Df	B	T	R	R^2	P
Internality–Externality	14,132	0.95	2.36	0.56	0.32	0.01
Risk-taking	14,132	0.70	2.96	–	–	0.01
Futurity	14,132	0.62	1.60	–	–	ns
Markets	14,132	0.38	1.45	–	–	ns
Planning and managing	14,132	0.38	0.80	–	–	ns
Heterogeneity	14,132	0.23	1.55	–	–	ns
Work overload	14,132	-0.25	1.27	–	–	ns
Dynamism	14,132	-0.21	1.45	–	–	ns
Innovation	14,132	0.23	1.09	–	–	ns
Social life	14,132	-0.20	0.84	–	–	ns
Proactivity	14,132	0.23	0.79	–	–	ns
Scanning	14,132	-0.10	0.73	–	–	ns
Work	14,132	0.22	0.65	–	–	ns
Differentiation	14,132	-0.10	0.07	–	–	ns
Technocratization	14,132	0.01	0.06	–	–	ns

Df=Degree of Freedom; B=Standardized regression weights; T=T Ratio; R=Multiple Correlation; P=Level of Significance.

Table 6.6: Regression Analysis for Internality-Oriented Managers.
Dependent Variable: Role Perceptions

Predictors	Df	B	T	R	R^2	P
Futurity	13,114	1.05	2.93	0.57	0.32	.01
Risk-taking	13,114	0.44	1.50	–	–	ns
Planning and managing	13.114	0.41	1.12	–	–	ns
Markets	13,114	0.34	0.92	–	–	ns
Scanning	13,114	-0.14	0.94	–	–	ns
Social life	13,114	-0.39	0.72	–	–	ns
Heterogeneity	13,114	0.08	0.48	–	–	ns
Work	13,114	-0.08	0.25	–	–	ns
Innovation	13,114	-0.07	0.34	–	–	ns
Technocratization	13,114	0.09	0.33	–	–	ns
Futurity	13,114	0.09	0.28	–	–	ns
Differentiation	13,114	0.02	0.16	–	–	ns
Dynamism	13,114	0.01	0.10	–	–	ns
Work overload	13,114	-0.03	0.05	–	–	ns

Df=Degree of Freedom; B=Standardized regression weights; T=T Ratio; R=Multiple Correlation; P=Level of Significance.

Table 6.7: Regression Analysis for Externality-Oriented Managers.
Dependent Variable: Role Perceptions

Predictors	Df	B	T	R	R^2	P
Differentiation	13,126	1.19	2.44	0.55	0.30	0.01
Innovation	13,126	0.82	2.23	–	–	0.05
Work overload	13,126	0.56	2.14	–	–	0.05
Planning and managing	13,126	0.70	2.11	–	–	0.05
Scanning	13,126	-0.26	1.55	–	–	ns
Social life	13,126	-0.13	1.32	–	–	ns
Markets	13,126	0.32	1.29	–	–	ns
Risk-taking	13,126	-0.32	1.14	–	–	ns
Dynamism	13,126	0.10	0.63	–	–	ns
Technocratization	13,126	0.15	0.52	–	–	ns
Heterogeneity	13,126	0.10	0.56	–	–	ns
Futurity	13,126	0.06	0.61	–	–	ns
Proactivity	13,126	-0.13	0.40	–	–	ns
Work	13,126	0.09	0.21	–	–	ns

Df=Degree of Freedom; B=Standardized regression weights; T=T Ratio; R=Multiple Correlation; P=Level of Significance.

The activity of planning and managing, and the use of the strategies of futurity, innovation, and risk-taking by managers are meaningful predictors in both sectors. Additionally, the differentiation aspect of structure, work overload and the internality-externality orientation are meaningful in the public sector, and dynamism in the environment, the time spent on work and the heterogeneity aspect of structure are meaningful in the private sector.

Dynamism in environment is significant in the loss-making group and the internality-externality orientation and the risk-taking strategy are significant in the profit-making corporations. The futurity strategy, the planning activity and the frequency of taking work home have all made substantial contribution. The knowledge of market trends and the use of risk-taking strategy are unique to the profit-making corporations, and the differentiation aspect of structure and the innovation strategy are unique to the loss-making corporations. The activity of planning and managing, the strategies of futurity and risk-taking and the knowledge of market trends have contributed substantially to the clarity of the internality-oriented managers, and work overload, the differentiation aspect of structure, the planning and managing activity, the innovation strategy and the time spent on social activities have contributed substantially to the clarity of the externality-oriented managers.

It emerges in substance that the clarity in role perceptions of managers depends to a certain extent on common variables, and to some extent on different variables. The private sector managers have the overriding job condition of relating to the owner(s) as direct employees and of identifying with the enterprise. The sense of personal commitment makes them put in more effort and spend more energy on discovering clear role definitions and responding to the variety of challenges in the environment. The public sector managers have, on the other hand, broad guidelines from the ministries concerned. They are given task of interpreting their roles in the given reality and providing meaningful orientations for themselves. The problem often experienced by them is not one of ambiguous role perceptions, but of manoeuvring the conditions and programmes to fit into the governmental policies. The challenge for them is to make new additions and adjustments in roles. To this end, the gaps in the domain of time management and strategy-making may provide some clues as to the nature of measures/interventions to be undertaken so that global and holistic thinking and the clarity in role perceptions of managers may be enhanced.

7

CONFIDENCE OF MANAGERS

Feeling Confident

The feeling of confidence is considered to be the opposite of the feeling of helplessness. The feeling of confidence is known to be reinforced by the sense that outcomes will relate to the responses made, and that one can control/intervene with contingencies to get the desired responses. The feeling of helplessness, on the other hand, may occur because of the feeling that responses will be independent of outcomes and that the contingencies are uncontrollable.

In recent years researchers have emphasized the importance of the relationship between perceived control and actual performance in diverse areas of functioning, individual and collective. Theorists have argued that when persons are asked to solve a problem that is actually not solvable, they learn that outcomes are non-contingent on their responses, and thus non-controllable (Abramson, Seligman and Teasdale, 1978; Maier and Seligman, 1976). In the event of these persons generalizing their perceptions of non-controllability to the subsequent problems they face, they would feel less confident of solving the problem and put in less effort, resulting in lower level of performance (less confident → less effort → lower performance).

Managers' feelings of loss of confidence or helplessness have been differentiated by their use of strategies. The helpless managers frequently use passive, conservative and reactive strategies; those who are confident adopt innovative, proactive and risky strategies in decision-making (Miller and Toulouse, 1986). It has been observed by Kahn (1990b) that managers as authority figures should give to their juniors the feeling that they themselves are competent and secure enough in their own visions to create paths along which the juniors can safely travel.

Managers' sensitivity to people and situations and their styles of interaction symbolize the extent of integration into the organizational system, internalization of responsibilities, acceptance of challenges, positive perceptions of co-workers and preparedness for changes in the patterns of power distribution. These reflect their feelings of confidence as persons and performers of whatever tasks they undertake. A higher degree of confidence in what they can do should negate any ambivalence in their relations with their chairmen-cum-managing directors and controlling ministries on the one hand, and with their subordinates on the other, by helping them in seeking their goals, and by taking head on the challenges that may otherwise threaten the achievement of goals. A demonstration of confidence in their ability to manage the units under their control effectively would earn them credibility and goodwill. Confidence in one's potential is known to breed action, and action in turn reinforces confidence.

In the corporate set-up, the position of senior managers places them at a selectively higher pedestal. By virtue of their position they interact with diverse types of persons/ groups, and have exposure to diverse situations and contingencies. Outside the organization, their origin happens to be in the higher social strata, where they have had continuity in their socialization at home and at school/college. They have, however, some gaps in terms of their preparation to cope with the contingencies of the organization. They can identify with the chosen few who are similar to them, but not with a sizeable number of those who constitute the supervisory staff and the rank and file of the employees. They often experience a gap in communicating with and in appreciating the needs of these supervisors/semi-skilled and unskilled employees. This leads to cognitive–affective blocks in their relating to the junior staff within the organization, and unpreparedness and avoidance of sharing of power with their co-workers, who happen to be less or equally qualified than them, but are placed at a lower rung in the hierarchy.

In the prevailing socio-political environment in the country, employees at almost all levels are unionized, and issues of equality, fair treatment and social justice have become important. Managers lack confidence in handling diverse types of groups and situations. The lack of confidence and goodwill between employees and management has increasingly encouraged the juniors to indulge in inappropriate behaviour on the pretext of slightest provocation. The juniors have not been able to develop a sense of identity or belonging, either with managers or/and with the organizations they work for. They tend to adopt more often than not aggressive dysfunctional strategies and tactics of operation. This makes the demonstration of a higher confidence in doing the job, a higher sensitivity towards people, and a clear vision of change particularly relevant for managers in the public sector in India, as employees in this sector come from diverse regions, and have high expectations of the system, and the managers.

The public sector corporations are much more complex organizations and have inevitably some coherent and some contradictory goals. The strategic management of these requires that managers should read the signals in the dynamic and turbulent environment (political, social, economic) speedily and accurately and act upon these efficiently. Success in doing so would indicate their competence and would further enhance their confidence in handling future contingencies, and in accomplishing the desired outcomes. The repeated failures of managers in achieving the desired outcomes, on the other hand, would induce a loss of perceived control and a sense of helplessness among them.

Although many researchers have considered trust and confidence as important personal attributes of able and good managers, they have not focused on helplessness or confidence in corporate set-up as an outcome variable. Khanna and Subramanian (1982) have observed with reference to the development administration in India that poor teamwork, pervasive feelings of powerlessness, targetry and status-orientation are the important causes of cost overruns and delays, citizen alienation, poor achievement of results and apathy. The feeling of confidence of managers has thus been analyzed as an outcome of personal and organizational attributes.

Operationalization and Measure

Confidence has been operationalized in terms of the overall control experienced by managers in their situation. The control could have either an internal or external locus and thus relate to the situation of work, the contents of work, or the manager's own capacity to manage the contingencies. Confidence has been measured here globally as well as specifically by referring to the authority, the organization and the various groups in these. This has been measured by 13 items/statements focusing on the contingencies of general and specific managerial functions. The functions are: the ability to resolve conflicts at work; to deal with seniors, juniors and peers; to solve problems within the unit; to meet standards of performance; and to resolve crisis situations like disagreements with the top executives and unions.

The statements are rated on a five-point scale ranging between 20 per cent and below to 80 per cent and above. The minimum score on the scale is 13 and the maximum score is 65. On pretesting, the scale had a Cronbach Alpha of 0.78 for the sample.

Managers' Confidence Levels

In all the groups, managers rated their confidence between 80-100 per cent and had mean confidence scores significantly higher than the theoretically expected mean (a score of 39 in the range of 13 to 65), negating the common assertion that numerous external controls and lack of supportive legislation have made managers helpless in organizational reality.

Managers in the private sector displayed a significantly higher degree of confidence than those in the public sector (M=55.89, SD=6.94; M=53.23, SD=6.12; t=2.44, p<0.05), indicating that the former are relatively less constrained in their choice of actions, have more freedom and flexibility in implementation, have direct accountability to the owner, and have less procedural restrictions in encountering the people and rewarding the outcomes. Some differences are found on specific items: 'in a situation of problems with the top administration', 'in overcoming troubles in my unit', 'when faced with disagreements with the top executive' and 'when faced with disagreements with labour unions'. On one item: 'in a situation of problems with the top administration', the private sector managers score close to the theoretical mean. The public sector managers score lower than the theoretical mean on two items: 'in overcoming troubles in my unit' and 'when faced with disagreements with the top executive'.

Within the public sector, the managers of the profit-making corporations display slightly higher level of confidence than those in the loss-making corporations, although the difference is of one point only and not significant (M=53.68, SD=6.95; M=52.68, SD=6.66). The internality-oriented managers show significantly higher confidence than the externality-oriented (M=54.18, SD=6.94; M=52.36, SD=6.62; t=2.20, p<0.05), indicating that the attributes of inner strength and ability are closely linked to confidence. In the loss-making corporations, the confidence of the more professionally committed managers has also been lower as they are forced to spend much of their time in fire-fighting operations, and in containing and evading further deterioration and losses, as these had constantly threatened their confidence in coping with the situation adequately.

The confidence of managers is associated with their internality in all the groups, but significantly for the public sector (0.19) and the profit-making group (r=0.26), indicating that the internals demonstrated greater confidence in their ability and actions than the externals did. In all the groups, the confidence of managers is significantly associated with goal achievement, indicating that irrespective of the differences in organizational structures, the conditions of operation and personal orientation directly help one's confidence in achieving the predetermined goals. The more confident managers can handle the contingencies and the ongoing situations with less stress. This has also been found true in relation to clarity in role perceptions and professional commitment (Table 7.1). Those who are confident of themselves have clearer role perceptions and vice versa. It should thus be necessary to understand what one is required to do, and what is expected in the complex organizational reality, to be able to feel that one can do it well. The highly confident managers are also the more professionally committed and have the needed skills at their disposal.

Table 7.1: Correlations of Confidence with Goal Achievement, Role Perceptions, Professional Commitment, Strategy, Environment and Structure

Variables	Pu	Pr	PM	LM	I	E
GA	0.39**	0.31*	0.36**	0.41**	0.40**	0.38**
RP	0.69**	0.90**	0.68**	0.70**	0.68**	0.69**
PC	0.56**	0.67**	0.51**	0.61**	0.57**	0.54**
I	0.15**	0.25	0.09	0.22**	0.14	0.15
RT	-0.10	-0.11	-0.13	0.04	0.00	-0.14
PA	0.18*	0.07	0.13	0.23**	0.17*	0.19*
F	0.31**	0.29*	0.37**	0.21*	0.36**	0.24**
D	0.11	-0.26	0.09	0.15	-0.01	0.20*
H	0.07	0.10	0.14	0.00	0.15	0.10
S	0.13	0.14	0.12	0.15	0.11	0.14
T	0.04	-0.03	0.11	-0.03	0.07	0.01
Di	0.20**	-0.06	0.30**	0.10	0.17*	0.22**

* $p < 0.05$
** $p < 0.01$

GA=Goal Achievement; RP=Role perceptions; PC=Professional Commitment; I=Innovation; RT=Risk-taking; PA=Proactivity; F=Futurity; D=Dynamism; H=Heterogeneity; S=Scanning; T=Technocratization; D=Differentiation; PM=Profit-Making; LM=Loss-Making; Pr=Private, Pu=Public; I=Internals, E=Externals.

Time Management

The time allocated by managers to different areas of life and the way they distribute their time for different work activities are differentially associated with their level of confidence. In the public sector, among the profit- and loss-making corporations, as well as for the internality- and externality-oriented managers, the time spent by managers in meeting their social obligations enhances their confidence. The coefficients of correlation range between -0.12 and 0.19 and some are statistically significant. The time spent on work as such generates self-confidence among managers in the public and private sectors, and within the former among managers of loss-making corporations and externality-oriented managers. The correlation has in fact been quite high ($r = 0.23$) for the externality-oriented managers.

The more confident managers in the private sector consider the time spent in meetings as a wastage of time. This is contrary to how managers in the public sector view the time spent in meetings.

This is seen in a negative correlation in the case of the former. Discussions with superiors and the knowledge of market trends have been found reassuring by managers in the private and public sectors and in profit-making corporations and by internals and externals. The frequency of work taken home has been important for the more confident managers in the private sector, in the loss-making corporations and the externality-oriented managers. In these groups the correlations range between 0.23 and 0.35. The activities of planning, managing and paperwork appear to have some meaning as a source of evading helplessness, for the more confident public sector managers, although the correlations are not significant. The more confident managers in the loss-making and externality-oriented groups in the public sector spend significantly more time in sorting out matters with the ministry officials, demonstrating the stronghold of the government on the public sector. In fact, they indulge in a variety of activities which are not relevant to their roles in the corporations, as shown by the highly significant correlation with unscheduled activities (r=0.42).

The time managed in various areas of life and the frequency of work taken home can explain the nine per cent variance in the confidence of managers in the public sector, and 17 per cent variance for managers in the private sector. These variables explain about five per cent of variance for the managers of profit-making corporations and the internality-oriented managers, 20 per cent for the managers of loss-making corporations and 12 per cent for the externality-oriented managers. The work overload, time spent on social life, and time given to hobbies are meaningful predictors of confidence for managers in the public sector and in the profit-making corporations. The time spent on family, sleeping and personal care can predict the confidence of managers in the private sector, while the time spent on hobbies, work, family and work overload predict the confidence of managers in the loss-making corporations. These variables are of positive value and relevant for managers in the public sector, profit- and loss-making corporations and for externality-oriented managers. They are of negative value for managers of the private sector and internality-oriented managers. Thus, while the confidence of public sector managers shows a strong direct base in the work domain, the private sector managers' confidence comes from time given to work. This is further complemented by spending time on family matters and on themselves. The managers who have a higher degree of inner strength feel confident when they avoid the cultivation of interpersonal relations. The externality-oriented managers desire to spend extra time on their work much more frequently.

The time allocated to various work activities can lead to differences in the confidence of managers. It can explain about nine per cent of variance for managers in the public sector, 29 per cent for managers in the private sector, nine per cent for managers the profit-making corporations, 15 per cent for managers in the loss-making corporations, five per cent for the internality-oriented managers and 23 per cent for the externality-oriented managers. The frequency of work taken home and the knowledge of market trends are important in the confidence of managers in the public sector, and the time spent on planning and discussions with superiors are important for managers in the private sector.

The more confident managers in the profit- and loss-making corporations take work home with significant frequency. They also spend more time on activities like acquiring knowledge of market trends, taking inspection rounds of workplaces, paperwork in the profit-making corporations, sorting out matters with the ministry officials and discussions with juniors and peers. Additionally, the activity of planning and managing is important in the loss-making corporations. While no particular activity is really found significant for the externality-oriented managers, the frequency of taking work home and the other activities are given equal attention. The internality-oriented managers in general manage to complete their work in the allocated time.

Strategy-Making, Environment and Structure

The use of the proactivity and futurity strategies and the differentiation aspect of structure are found significantly associated with the confidence of public sector managers, while the risk-taking strategy and the technocratization aspect of structure are not found significantly useful by any group (Table 7.1). Since most public sector corporations are large, hierarchical and managed in a bureaucratic fashion, the managers are required to take only low risks. Also, no corporate managers found the implementation of proposals involving high degree of technocratization difficult. It has been felt that all managers having higher confidence display higher personal commitment, and higher futurity-orientation in coping with problems and challenges in their jobs.

The confidence of managers in the profit-making group is associated with professional commitment, the futurity strategy and the differentiation aspect of structure. In the loss-making group, the managers' confidence correlates with the innovation, proactivity and futurity strategies. Strategy-making is associated with the confidence of managers in the loss-making corporations more than in the profit-making corporations. Other meaningful variables for the loss-making corporations are dynamism in the environment and the scanning and differentiation aspects of structure.

The confidence scores of the internality- as well as the externality-oriented managers are positively associated with proactivity and futurity strategies and the differentiation aspect of structure. Although the innovation strategy, heterogeneity in the environment and the scanning aspect of structure emerge as meaningful, the correlations are not significant. Dynamism in the environment has been found to be a significant reinforcement of the confidence of externality-oriented managers. This perhaps provides compensatory stimuli to them and enhances their inner strength and ability.

The strategy-making, environment and structure variables explain about 14 per cent of variance in the confidence of managers in the public sector and 37 per cent in the private sector enterprises. Futurity and proactivity strategies and the differentiation aspect of structure are important in the case of the public sector. Futurity strategy and heterogeneity in the environment are meaningful for the private sector. Both the strategy-making and environment variables are meaningful in the two sectors. The addition of internality–externality score to the above equation improved prediction for the public sector by two per cent. The prediction for the private sector has not improved, however. These variables explain the level of confidence of managers to the level of 20 per cent for the profit-making corporations and 12 per cent for the loss-making corporations. The meaningful predictors for the profit-making corporations are futurity, innovation and proactivity strategies, and the differentiation aspect of structure. Same is true for the loss-making corporations. The addition of internality–externality score to the equation yields improved prediction by four per cent for the profit-making corporations and no gain for the loss-making corporations.

The futurity strategy helps significantly in instilling confidence in internality-oriented managers. Greater differentiation of structures and low risk-taking are desired by externality-oriented managers. Environmental variables prove insignificant in predicting confidence of managers in both groups. The two groups perhaps use strategies differently to be able to act with confidence.

Composite Trends

The selected variables of time management, strategy-making, environment and structure predict the confidence of managers to the maximum of 35 per cent in the public sector (Table 7.2), 58 per cent in the private sector (Table 7.3), 40 per cent each for the loss- and profit-making corporations (Tables 7.4, 7.5), 34 per cent for the internality-oriented managers (Table 7.6) and 46 per cent for the externality-oriented managers (Table 7.7).

Table 7.2: Regression Analysis for Public Sector Enterprises.
Dependent Variable: Confidence

Predictors	Df	B	T	R	R^2	P
Work overload	16,251	1.12	2.91	0.59	0.35	0.01
Social life	16,251	1.05	2.64	–	–	0.01
Futurity	16,251	0.91	2.39	–	–	0.01
Internality–Externality	16,251	0.73	1.86	–	–	0.10
Differentiation	16,251	0.54	1.83	–	–	0.10
Hobbies	16,251	0.40	1.67	–	–	ns
Heterogeneity	16,251	0.41	1.63	–	–	ns
Risk-taking	16,251	0.30	1.57	–	–	ns
Innovation	16,251	0.24	1.47	–	–	ns
Ministry	16,251	-0.16	1.43	–	–	ns
Residuals	16,251	-0.11	0.93	–	–	ns
Dynamism	16,251	0.07	0.61	–	–	ns
Markets	16,251	-0.18	0.31	–	–	ns
Scanning	16,251	-0.04	0.31	–	–	ns
Proactivity	16,251	-0.06	0.24	–	–	ns
Technocratization	16,251	-0.02	0.11	–	–	ns
Work	16,251	-0.02	0.05	–	–	ns

Df=Degree of Freedom; B=Standardized regression weights; T=T Ratio; R=Multiple Correlation; P=Level of Significance.

Table 7.3: Regression Analysis for Private Sector Enterprises.
Dependent Variable: Confidence

Predictors	Df	B	T	R	R^2	P
Innovation	13,32	1.05	3.16	0.76	0.58	0.01
Residual	13,32	0.81	2.12	–	–	0.05
Dynamism	13,32	0.80	2.08	–	–	0.05
Heterogeneity	13,32	0.79	1.99	–	–	0.10
Internality–Externality	13,32	0.51	1.02	–	–	ns
Futurity	13,32	0.51	1.59	–	–	ns
Risk-taking	13,32	-0.43	1.43	–	–	ns
Work	13,32	-0.42	1.47	–	–	ns
Differentiation	13,32	-0.34	1.22	–	–	ns
Work overload	13,32	-0.26	1.13	–	–	ns
Proactivity	13,32	-0.19	0.89	–	–	ns
Social life	13,32	-0.21	0.87	–	–	ns
Scanning	13,32	-0.13	0.69	–	–	ns
Ministry	13,32	-0.10	0.06	–	–	ns

Df=Degree of Freedom; B=Standardized regression weights; T=T Ratio; R=Multiple Correlation; P=Level of Significance.

Table 7.4: Regression Analysis for Loss-Making Corporations.
Dependent Variable: Confidence

Predictors	Df	B	T	R	R^2	P
Work overload	16,104	1.20	2.53	0.63	0.40	0.01
Innovation	16,104	0.80	2.02	–	–	0.05
Social life	16,104	0.62	1.97	–	–	0.05
Dynamism	16,104	0.37	1.63	–	–	ns
Ministry	16,104	0.35	1.27	–	–	ns
Differentiation	16,104	0.31	1.30	–	–	ns
Risk-taking	16,104	0.26	0.84	–	–	ns
Proactivity	16,104	0.25	0.68	–	–	ns
Scanning	16,104	0.23	0.56	–	–	ns
Heterogeneity	16,104	0.15	0.75	–	–	ns
Internality-Externality	16,104	0.11	0.52	–	–	ns
Futurity	16,104	0.10	0.38	–	–	ns
Residual	16,104	0.04	0.27	–	–	ns
Work	16,104	0.13	0.22	–	–	ns
Markets	16,104	-0.06	0.11	–	–	ns
Superiors	16,104	0.08	0.11	–	–	ns
Technocratization	16,104	-0.03	0.09	–	–	ns

Df=Degree of Freedom; B=Standardized regression weights; T=T Ratio; R=Multiple Correlation; P=Level of Significance.

Table 7.5: Regression Analysis for Profit-Making Corporations.
Dependent Variable: Confidence

Predictors	Df	B	T	R	R^2	P
Internality–Externality	17,129	1.07	3.08	0.64	0.40	0.01
Futurity	17,129	1.04	2.45	–	–	0.01
Superiors	17,129	0.74	1.82	–	–	0.01
Work overload	17,129	0.69	1.79	–	–	0.10
Hobbies	17,129	0.51	1.86	–	–	0.10
Social life	17,129	0.44	1.48	–	–	ns
Heterogeneity	17,129	0.43	1.36	–	–	ns
Risk-taking	17,129	0.37	1.36	–	–	ns
Residuals	17,129	0.30	1.25	–	–	ns
Ministry	17,129	-0.22	1.12	–	–	ns
Differentiation	17,129	-0.16	0.76	–	–	ns
Scanning	17,129	0.10	0.68	–	–	ns
Market	17,129	-0.38	0.50	–	–	ns
Dynamism	17,129	0.07	0.40	–	–	ns
Technocratization	17,129	-0.05	0.19	–	–	ns
Proactivity	17,129	-0.02	0.05	–	–	ns
Innovation	17,129	0.01	0.02	–	–	ns
Work	17,129	0.01	0.01	–	–	ns

Df=Degree of Freedom; B=Standardized regression weights; T=T Ratio; R=Multiple Correlation; P=Level of Significance.

Table 7.6: Regression Analysis for Internality-Oriented Managers.
Dependent Variable: Confidence

Predictors	Df	B	T	R	R^2	P
Futurity	16,111	0.85	2.56	0.58	0.34	0.01
Social life	16,111	0.59	1.68	–	–	0.10
Hobbies	16,111	0.50	1.27	–	–	ns
Superiors	16,111	0.41	0.99	–	–	ns
Ministry	16,111	0.39	1.36	–	–	ns
Dynamism	16,111	0.34	0.72	–	–	ns
Innovation	16,111	0.30	1.07	–	–	ns
Differentiation	16,111	0.19	0.44	–	–	ns
Heterogeneity	16,111	0.13	0.66	–	–	ns
Work	16,111	-0.22	0.49	–	–	ns
Markets	16,111	-0.35	0.38	–	–	ns
Work overload	16,111	0.28	0.39	–	–	ns
Technocratization	16,111	0.09	0.23	–	–	ns
Residual	16,111	-0.16	0.23	–	–	ns
Scanning	16,111	0.04	0.22	–	–	ns
Proactivity	16,111	0.01	0.03	–	–	ns
Risk Taking	16,111	-0.33	1.09	–	–	ns

Df=Degree of Freedom; B=Standardized regression weights; T=T Ratio; R=Multiple Correlation; P=Level of Significance.

Table 7.7: Regression Analysis for Externality-Oriented Managers.
Dependent Variable: Confidence

Predictors	Df	B	T	R	R^2	P
Work overload	16,123	1.15	4.24	0.68	0.46	0.01
Innovation	16,123	1.07	3.15	–	–	0.01
Differentiation	16,123	1.01	2.36	–	–	0.01
Social life	16,123	0.93	1.67	–	–	0.10
Risk-taking	16,123	0.61	1.57	–	–	ns
Residual	16,123	0.56	1.34	–	–	ns
Dynamism	16,123	0.27	0.46	–	–	ns
Technocratization	16,123	0.15	0.59	–	–	ns
Futurity	16,123	0.06	0.57	–	–	ns
Scanning	16,123	-0.09	0.60	–	–	ns
Markets	16,123	-0.18	0.25	–	–	ns
Superiors	16,123	-0.25	0.35	–	–	ns
Hobbies	16,123	-0.18	0.32	–	–	ns
Work	16,123	-0.10	0.24	–	–	ns
Heterogeneity	16,123	0.02	0.10	–	–	ns
Proactivity	16,123	-0.02	0.06	–	–	ns
Ministry	16,123	-0.02	0.02	–	–	ns

Df=Degree of Freedom; B=Standardized regression weights; T=T Ratio; R=Multiple Correlation; P=Level of Significance.

The futurity strategy, work overload, social life, the differentiation aspect of structure, and internality–externality are meaningful in the public sector. The innovation strategy, dynamism and heterogeneity in the environment and the time on residual activities are meaningful in the private sector.

The meaningful predictors of managers' confidence in profit-making corporations are the futurity strategy, internality, work overload, the time spent on discussions with superiors and hobbies. The confidence of managers in loss-making corporations is best predicted by the frequency of taking work home, the innovation strategy and the time spent on social activities. Thus, in case of both types of corporations, while some predictors are common, managers use different strategies. This is an expected finding. The futurity strategy and the time spent on social life are significant for the internality-oriented managers, and the frequency of work taken home, the innovation strategy and the differentiation aspect of structure are significant for the externality-oriented managers. Social life is only marginally relevant.

Inferences

It thus seems possible to infer that the personal and organizational variables are relatively more relevant for the confidence of managers in the private sector and for the externality-oriented managers than for the other groups. The frequency of taking work home has been an important time variable in the public sector, profit- and loss-making corporations and externality-oriented group, while the time spent on social obligations has been useful for managers in the private sector, loss-making corporations and internality- and externality-oriented group. The time given to hobbies and discussions with superiors is found to bolster the confidence of the profit-making group. The confident managers use the futurity strategy in the public sector, profit-making corporations and internality-oriented group. The use of the innovation strategy is made in the private sector, loss-making corporations and externality-oriented group. The dynamism and heterogeneity aspects of environment affect the confidence of managers in the private sector. The differentiation aspect of structure is used by the public sector and externality-oriented managers. The internality of managers has been relevant for the confidence of managers in the public sector and those in the profit-making corporations.

Different groups of managers tend to perceive and value the same variables differently. The managers in the public sector, profit-making corporations and internality-oriented group use the futurity strategy to enhance their confidence in coping with realities, while the private sector, loss-making corporations and externality-oriented managers use more of the innovation strategy for the purpose. The turbulence in the environment is relevant for managers in the private sector as they find the policies and practices of the government to be shifting, ambiguous and negotiable under pressure at all levels. The public sector and the externality-oriented managers find the diversification of units and products helpful in increasing their confidence. They always show this to the government as achievement. The recurrent failure of the loss-making corporations to achieve the targets lowers their confidence, and makes the relation between their actions and consequences imperceptible. They even fail to use the relevant information in decision-making and suffer from lack of results in performance. It thus emerges as a policy prescription that the controlling ministries ought to guard against excessive controls and negative reinforcements, as the situation in the public sector is slowly moving towards a desperate end.

A high level of confidence is demonstrated by managers in the private sector on account of their greater freedom of action, flexibility and opportunities of discussions with superiors and their frequent use of the innovation strategy. The reverse seems to be the case in the public sector as these operate under conditions of diffused autonomy, set procedures and rules, and meaningless attendance at meetings, especially the lengthy meetings for the sake of joint participation without achieving any results. Managers in the public sector experience lack of control, a consequent lack of confidence, and a feeling of helplessness. Such feelings are further reinforced from contextual factors such as demeaning social labels (weak and spineless management), tasks or work setting (Langer and Benevento, 1978), and from comparative observations and/or information about the experiences of similar referents in well-functioning corporations (Bandura, 1977; Devellis, McEvoy Devellis and McCauley, 1978). The achievement of planned goals should reinforce confidence, but frequently such attempts are thwarted by multiple controls and vested interests. The goals often become illusory and unrealistic. While it seems true that the information about the challenges faced by corporations and the need to set exciting and realistic work goals would motivate the managers to put in the desired time, effort and ability, the setting of goals externally and unrealistically can be demotivating and could adversely affect their confidence. The tight controls in the environment, such as close supervision by ministries in the case of the public sector and particularly so in the loss-making group, curb intrinsic motivation and stifle the initiative and confidence of managers (Kohn, 1976). Further, all managers who show higher levels of confidence do not have similar perceptions of the problems and the causes. Some refuse to accept the shortcomings of their corporations, some accept and yet ignore them. Then there are managers who admit of poor performance and lack of results, and yet show outwardly high confidence. It may be argued by using the elements of the cognitive interference interpretation (Coyne, Metalsky and Lavelle, 1980) that some managers, such as those in the loss-making corporations who face unsolvable problems and difficulties on multiple counts, have a tendency of excessive engagement in self-centred thoughts, which leads to lack of performance results on a recurrent basis. This may be a reflection on their attempts to distance themselves from the current situation which is demotivating, passive and devoid of challenges (Mikulincer, 1989). It may be that some managers show unrealistic optimism because of their affective and cognitive predispositions and thus higher confidence, even when they are not able to achieve, what they desire. The personality correlates of confidence in one's decisions have been investigated by Wolfe and Grosch (1990). They find that confidence ratings show a consistent pattern of individual differences.

The conventional prescriptions suggested for bolstering the level of confidence or for minimizing helplessness include realistic job reviews, the setting of specific and challenging goals, prompt and balanced feedback, conditional reinforcement, appropriate role models and the removal of excessive controls etc. Indeed, what Sutton and Kahn (1987) have advocated seems to be useful. The managers should use the available feedback system effectively to obtain information, to enhance their intrinsic motivation, and have an opportunity to draw their own inferences and develop a sense of preparedness to cope with the challenges and constraints. This would help them to feel confident and enhance their feeling of achievement.

8

Professional Commitment

Commitment: Its Connotations

The term 'commitment' has been used in the literature on organizations to describe diverse phenomena such as the willingness of social actors to give their energy and loyalty to social systems (Kanter, 1968), an awareness of the impossibility of choosing a differential social identity or of rejecting a particular expectation under force of penalty (Stebbins, 1970), and the binding of an individual to behavioural acts (Salancik, 1977). The term has also been used in different contexts in different organizations and professions. Organizational commitment has been the focus of the social exchange theory of Homans (1958) and the side bet theory of Becker (1960). The two theories are not mutually exclusive as both consider organizational commitment as a structural phenomenon. Contrary to this, professional commitment refers to the higher order technical skills on the part of the individual and to the faith and intent to conform to the norms of the profession as prescribed on a consensual basis by the professional bodies in a standard manner so as not to allow people to indulge in deviant and unethical practices and to bring disrepute to the profession. Professional commitment requires a person to accept his/her responsibilities as member of the specific profession vis-à-vis other members of the professional group, and to practise the profession to earn a better image/respectability for the professional group and the profession. A professional qualification imposes a commitment on a person and is known to be a vertical differentiating mechanism in organizations where persons having higher qualifications are placed in higher positions which carry more responsibility, and have to behave in ways that would befit the professional category they belong to.

Numerous management experts and practitioners have argued that managers occupying senior and top-level positions in the organizational hierarchy have a very high degree of technical competence and competitiveness, the capability to do the job in a professional manner, the responsibility of helping their subordinates to develop, the ability to innovate, and the willingness to earn a reputation for the profession as well as for the organization. They are expected to demonstrate a high degree of commitment to the profession and the organization. This double-edged expectation continues to be a puzzle for managers and researchers. It is not clear whether the role expectations of the senior managers contain contradictions which restrain them from achieving one, while being successful in the other, or vice versa. Technically, it seems that professional commitment should get priority, as the managers are socialized into the norms of the profession and are trained to do that, while in practice organizational commitment frequently gets priority because of one's commitment to the service contract itself. Managers attempt to maintain a balance between professional and organizational expectations and perform efficaciously. This often causes psychological conflicts and ambivalence in their decision-making, and adversely affects their effectiveness.

Senior managers are pressurized to translate professional as well as organizational commitments into positive actions leading to individual and corporate performance of a high order. They often find, however, that the two cannot be accomplished to an equal extent. The possibility of a conflict between professional and organizational commitment has also been reported by Knapp (1962). A positive attitude towards change of job, leader and organizational unit is reported to have a negative influence on commitment (Stevens, Beyer and Trice, 1978). One can surmise that the higher the professional commitment of managers, the higher should be their effectiveness and the organizational performance. It is observed as well as feared that even the most competent managers, after they have worked for several years in an organization, may find it difficult to manage their professional commitment positively. The probability would be still higher if the organizational policies and practices are not supportive of professionalism. The rational and well-functioning organizations should value the professional commitment of managers and create conducive conditions to practise and reinforce it. The organizations are thus required to recruit competency-based managers, and then socialize them into professional and organizational norms. This should help them to use formal and tacit knowledge and to act in a balanced way.

Managers displaying higher professional commitment, in addition to their ability and competence to make rational and informed decisions, are known to be guided by consensually determined norms of the profession. They are expected to be objective, fair and convincing to the organizations and the individual members in it. To the extent they would conform to the norms (professional or otherwise), their decisions may be externally constrained, but the interpretation of the situation and the conviction would largely be personal and subjectively determined. They would thus reflect a good mix of internality–externality, conformity, flexibility, adaptability, intent to preserve the standards and dynamism etc. They would be committed to professional norms and would be able to demonstrate a keen desire to cultivate such organizational practices and procedures as may enhance their personal and organizational effectiveness as managers.

Researches emanating from professionals, groups of scientists and engineers indicate that they have to confront unique issues (Kerr, Glinow and Schriesheim, 1977), and that professional commitment enhances individual productivity and cumulative productivity of organizations (Jauch, Glueck and Osborn, 1978). It has also been observed that it is not enough that one has professional skills and competence. One should have the additional ability to use these skills adequately and consistently under different conditions and to accomplish desired levels of outcomes. Managers who have the same type of training and professional preparation may perform differently, ranging from poor to extraordinary performance, depending on their own beliefs and convictions, their interpretations of roles, their ability to communicate and relate to others in the group, and their understanding of the context etc. How and to what extent would the professional skills or communication competencies of senior managers who are in different organizational settings and/or have different personal orientations affect their professional commitment? These questions need to be answered after careful research.

Professional Commitment and its Measure

Professional commitment is defined as one's faith and conscious intent to conform to the norms of the chosen profession. It has been assumed that the desire to contribute to the development of the profession would lead to a better image/respectability of the professional group. Managers in every society constitute a highly skilled group of people who are expected to adhere, in their day-to-day functioning, to prescribed professional standards. A deviance (volitional or otherwise) should cause conflict/ concern in them as persons and also in the group. How far senior managers in the public and private sector enterprises in India are able to demonstrate their professional commitment, and thus effectiveness, has been of interest here.

Professional commitment has been measured by an additive index of six items which reflect a manager's professional values. Each item has been rated on a five-point scale with regard to its importance to the manager (true to 20 per cent and below to 80 per cent and above) in his/her position in the organizational context. Jauch, Glueck and Obsorn (1978) have reported the mean index of professional commitment scale on researchers as 23.7 within a range of 9–30 (the possible range was 6–30). The split-half Spearman Brown internal reliability coefficient was 0.72. The use of the scale on a pre-tryout study on 15 managers yielded an inter-rater reliability of 0.82, which has been found to satisfy the required level of significance.

Professional Commitment of Managers

All senior managers demonstrate a very high level of professional commitment, as all of them scored significantly higher than the theoretical mean (M=18). There are no significant group differences in terms of sectoral identities (M=28.37, SD=2.63; M=27.55, SD=3.04), profit status of corporations (M=27.63, SD=2.95; M=27.46, SD=3.16) and personal orientations (M=27.79, SD=2.99; M=27.34, SD=3.08). The professionally committed and internality-oriented managers are more innovative than the professionally committed and externality-oriented managers. Further, managers in the profit-making group tend to take slightly more risks than those in the loss-making group. Managers in the public sector and within it those in the loss-making corporations are more active than those in the private sector and in profit-making public sector corporations. All managers are futurity-oriented, indicating that the professionally committed aim at better performance and are optimistic about their effectiveness. Those in the public sector, in the profit-making group, and those who are externality-oriented find diversification of structures to be a positive way of growth. Internals possess more occupationally relevant knowledge and thus greater professional commitment, according to some other researchers. The information processing capacity of internals is higher than that of the externals according to Lefcourt (1978).

Time Management

The time profiles of the professionally committed managers in different groups have many similarities, suggesting compatible demands experienced at their job level. There are also some differences which distinguish them from each other. The professional commitment of managers has been found negatively associated with the time spent on social life by all groups (correlations range between -0.19 and -0.27), except the private sector, indicating that either the more professionally committed are so preoccupied with numerous activities as part of the job that they do not have time for additional social obligations or that they consider these irrelevant and therefore consciously avoid spending time on them. The private sector managers, despite their professionalism, do spend some time on social obligations and a good deal of time in hobbies. Managers in the private and public sectors, and particularly the externality-oriented managers, conceive of hobbies as positive and constructive outlets, as seen by the positive associations with professional commitment. The association with time on family obligations is relevant only for the internality-oriented group. The time given to work has equal importance for the professional managers having externality and internality orientations. The time spent on sleeping and personal care has been of nominal relevance in all the groups except the private sector (r=-0.30). The importance of time perspectives in organizational involvement has also been noted by Darasse (1988).

In all the groups, professional commitment is significantly associated with planning and managing as an activity (the values of r range between 0.11 and 0.40), indicating that planning happens to be a general activity, in varying extent, of all professionally qualified managers. The knowledge of market trends has a positive salience for those in the public sector, for the internality-oriented, and for those in loss-making group, and a negative salience for the private sector group. The professionally committed managers in the private sector spend more time on discussions with superiors (r=0.23) than on discussions with juniors and peers (r=-0.29), meetings (r=-0.20), sorting out with ministry officials and unspecified activities. Those in the public sector spend more time on meetings and unspecified activities. Even the managers in the loss-making corporations spend less time on meetings and paperwork, if they score higher on professional commitment. The internality-oriented managers spend more time on discussions with juniors and peers, meetings and sorting out with ministry officials, while the externality-oriented managers spend more time on paperwork, meetings and residual activities. The highly professionally committed, who have external orientation and are in the loss-making group, see the putting in of extra time as a minimally expected positive practice. The frequency of work taken home is not very high in any group.

The time management variables can account for approximately seven per cent of variance in the professional commitment of managers in the public sector and about 19 per cent for managers in the private sector. For the public sector, the meaningful predictors have been the time spent on social life, frequency of work taken home and hobbies. The time spent on sleeping and personal care, which has a negative weight, is the only significant predictor for the private sector. The more professionally committed managers in the private sector prefer to spend less time on personal care.

The time allocated to various work activities explain variance in the professional commitment of managers in the public (11 per cent) and private (52 per cent) sectors to different extents. The significant predictors in the public sector are the activities of planning and meetings, against residual work activities and discussions with juniors and peers in the private sector. The more professionally committed managers in the public sector spend more time on planning and meetings, while such managers in the private sector do unspecified work and discuss little with peers and juniors to make them understand what is expected of them.

The time management variables account for variance in the professional commitment of managers in the profit- and loss-making corporations to different extents. Between the profit- and loss-making corporations, the time spent on work activities can explain about eight per cent of variance in the professional commitment of managers in the former, and 19 per cent of variance for the latter group. In the profit-making group the important activities are the activity of planning and discussions with peers and juniors. Also for the loss-making group, the time spent on meetings, paperwork and work taken home are important. The professionals in the profit-making group spend more time on planning and discussions with peers and juniors, as the responsibility of implementation of programmes and policies is collective. The development of subordinates is one of the expected obligations for them. Such managers in the loss-making group try to spend little more time on meetings and paperwork and even take work home quite frequently.

Time management in different areas of life accounted for 10 and eight per cent of variance respectively for the internality- and externality-oriented groups. For both, the time given to social activities has negative weights, and the time given to hobbies has positive weights. Additionally, for the internals the time given to the family is a positive predictor, indicating that family obligations distracted them. The time allocated to work activities predict 13 and 15 per cent of variance for the two groups respectively. The positive predictors of professional commitment of internals are discussions with juniors and peers, knowing about markets, sorting out with the ministries and planning and managing. Discussions with superiors and meetings are negative predictors of the professional commitment of externals. The work overload has a positive value. The time on meetings, paperwork, and residual activities have negative value.

Strategy-Making, Environment and Structure

The professional commitment of managers is related to only a few strategy-making, environment and structure variables in all the groups (Table 8.1). It is related positively to the futurity strategy in the public sector, in profit- and loss-making corporations and in internality-oriented managers; to the proactivity strategy in the public sector, in loss-making corporations and in internality-oriented managers; to dynamism in the environment negatively in the private but positively in the loss-making group; to heterogeneity in the environment in the public sector, in profit-making corporations and internality-oriented managers; and in the differentiation aspect of structure in the public sector and in profit-making corporations.

Table 8.1: Correlations of Professional Commitment with Goal Achievement, Role Perceptions, Confidence Strategy, Environment and Structure

Variables		Pu	Pr	PM	LM	I	E
GA		0.28**	0.33*	0.21**	0.34**	0.15*	0.20*
RP		0.56**	0.67**	0.51**	0.61**	0.29**	0.48**
C		0.55**	0.57*	0.60**	0.50**	0.16*	0.56**
I		0.11	0.19	0.09	0.13	0.20*	0.03
RT	Strategy	-0.10	0.18	0.16*	-0.03	-0.12	-0.07
PA		0.16*	0.19	0.04	0.30**	0.18*	0.15
F		0.20**	0.17	0.22**	0.19*	0.25**	0.15
D	Environment	0.11	-0.30	0.05	0.17*	0.09	0.13
H		0.14	0.19	0.18*	0.10	0.18*	0.12
S		0.06	0.05	0.02	0.15	0.07	0.03
T	Structure	0.13	-0.18	0.09	0.18*	0.24**	0.04
Di		0.16*	-0.01	0.27**	0.05	0.17*	0.14

* $p<0.05$
** $p<0.01$

GA=Goal Achievement; C=Confidence; PC=Professional commitment; I=Innovation; RT=Risk taking; PA=Proactivity; F=Futurity; D=Dynamism; H=Heterogeneity; S=Scanning; T=Technocratization; DI=Differentiation; PM=Profit-making; LM=Loss-Making; Pr=Private, Pu=Public; I=Internals, E=Externals.

The more professionally committed managers demonstrate more frequent and positive use of futurity- and activity-oriented strategies in the public sector, in profit and loss-making corporations and in internality-oriented group. Strategy-making has been more positively associated with professional commitment of managers in the public sector than in the private sector. The professionally committed managers in the public sector, and particularly in profit-making corporations and in internality-oriented group, perceive the environment as complex and filled with variety. They cope with these by evolving diversified structures. Those in the loss-making corporations and those who have internality-orientation find the technocratization aspect of structure more useful. Strategy-making reflects the professionalism of the managers in the public sector. The professionally committed managers in the private sector perceive the environment as having less challenge. The higher the professional commitment of managers, the less dynamic they find the environment. The more professionally committed display inner strength, confidence and the ability to manage their job in the organization. This may have been a concomitant of their training as well as their adherence to the norms of the profession. The environment for managers in the private sector has not been sufficiently dynamic from their perspective. The higher the professional commitment of managers, the less dynamic (and not moving positively) is the environment. The more professionally committed managers are also higher on internality, but the correlations are low in all groups.

The strategy making, environment and structure variables explain only 11 per cent of variance in the public sector and 29 per cent in the private sector. The meaningful predictors in the public sector are the futurity and risk-taking strategies, and heterogeneity in the environment, while the futurity strategy and heterogeneity in the environment are relevant in the private sector. The public as well as the private sector managers have positive futurity-orientation and a high capability to cope with diverse challenges in the environment, but the former make little use of the risk-taking strategy.

The strategy-making, the environment and structure variables accounted for 10 per cent variance for the profit-making group and 13 per cent for the loss-making group. For the profit-making group, the meaningful predictors are the differentiation aspect of structure, futurity and risk-taking strategies, and heterogeneity in the environment. For the loss-making group, the proactivity strategy is important. The addition of personal orientation does not make a difference to any group. Some strategy-making is relevant in both groups. It is futurity for the profit-making and proactivity strategy for the loss-making group. Additionally, for the former group some aspects of the environment and structure matter.

Composite Trends

There are differences on the basis of sector, profit status and individual personal orientation in the extent of managers' professional commitment being accounted for by the pooling together of selected predictors of time management, time spent on work activities, personal orientation, strategy, environment and structure.

The aspects of time management explain the variance in the professional commitment of managers to the extent of seven per cent for the public sector and 19 per cent for the private sector. The selected variables of time management, time spent on work activities, strategy-making, environment, structure and personal orientation explained a maximum of 65 per cent of variance for the private sector (Table 8.2) and 27 per cent for the public sector (Table 8.3).

Table 8.2: Regression Analysis for Private Sector Enterprises.
Dependent Variable: Professional Commitment

Predictors	Df	B	T	R	R^2	P
Planning and managing	17,28	1.02	3.53	0.81	0.65	0.01
Dynamism	17,28	0.86	2.75	–	–	0.01
Markets	17,28	0.55	1.58	–	–	ns
Proactivity	17,28	0.47	0.53	–	–	ns
Hobbies	17,28	0.31	1.26	–	–	ns
Internality–Externality	17,28	0.26	1.45	–	–	ns
Meetings	17,28	0.15	0.92	–	–	ns
Technocratization	17,28	0.12	0.67	–	–	ns
Differentiation	17,28	0.10	0.56	–	–	ns
Heterogeneity	17,28	-0.07	0.49	–	–	ns
Innovation	17,28	0.09	0.39	–	–	ns
Futurity	17,28	0.03	0.24	–	–	ns
Work overload	17,28	-0.22	0.44	–	–	ns
Work	17,28	0.11	0.30	–	–	ns
Social life	17,28	0.17	0.33	–	–	ns
Paperwork	17,28	0.11	0.23	–	–	ns
Scanning	17,28	0.02	0.10	–	–	ns
Risk-taking	17,28	-0.02	0.07	–	–	ns

Df=Degree of Freedom; B=Standardized regression weights; T=T Ratio; R=Multiple Correlation; P=Level of Significance.

More variance in the professional commitment of managers in the private sector has been explained by the variables of time management (19 per cent), time on work activities (52 per cent), strategy-making, environment and structure (29 per cent), separately as well as by the pooling together of relevant variables (65 per cent). For the private sector, the dynamism aspect of environment and the time spent on planning as a work activity are important. The meaningful predictors in the public sector are the time spent on social life and meetings, heterogeneity in the environment, the futurity and risk-taking strategy and the differentiation aspect of structure. The contextual variables and personal orientation are not very important. The aspects of strategy and structure, which are important for the public sector are not so for the private sector. Apparently the public sector is much less affected by the turbulence in the environment because the government decisions are taken to protect them, while the private sector is kept guessing and has to prepare in anticipation ways of coping with various challenges, by undertaking planning and managing activities, and by managing the dynamism in the environment.

Table 8.3: Regression Analysis for Public Sector Corporations.
Dependent Variable: Professional Commitment

Predictors	Df	B	T	R	R^2	P
Social life	17,250	1.08	3.60	0.52	0.27	0.01
Meetings	17,250	0.87	2.87	–	–	0.01
Work overload	17,250	0.86	2.78	–	–	0.01
Heterogeneity	17,250	0.77	2.12	–	–	0.05
Futurity	17,250	0.56	1.69	–	–	0.10
Differentiation	17,250	0.31	1.69	–	–	0.10
Paperwork	17,250	-0.19	1.21	–	–	ns
Technocratization	17,250	0.13	1.25	–	–	ns
Hobbies	17,250	0.22	1.05	–	–	ns
Risk-taking	17,250	-0.18	1.05	–	–	ns
Planning and managing	17,250	0.17	0.94	–	–	ns
Innovation	17,250	0.07	0.95	–	–	ns
Scanning	17,250	-0.06	1.17	–	–	ns
Proactivity	17,250	0.06	0.56	–	–	ns
Internality–Externality	17,250	-0.04	0.54	–	–	ns
Dynamism	17,250	0.01	0.20	–	–	ns
Work	17,250	0.02	0.16	–	–	ns
Markets	17,250	0.02	0.09	–	–	ns

Df=Degree of Freedom; B=Standardized regression weights; T=T Ratio; R=Multiple Correlation; P=Level of Significance.

The selected variables of time management, time spent on work activities, strategy, environment, structure and personal orientation explain a maximum of 24 per cent of variance for the profit-making corporations and 42 per cent of variance for the loss-making group. The results of the regression analysis are reported in Tables 8.4 and 8.5.

Table 8.4: Regression Analysis for Profit-Making Corporations.
Dependent Variable: Professional Commitment

Predictors	Df	B	T	R	R^2	P
Differentiation	12,133	0.65	1.93	0.49	0.24	0.10
Heterogeneity	12,133	0.57	1.89	–	–	0.10
Planning and managing	12,133	0.32	1.16	–	–	ns
Risk-taking	12,133	-0.19	1.49	–	–	ns
Work overload	12,133	-0.41	1.21	–	–	ns
Internality–Externality	12,133	-0.37	1.24	–	–	ns
Innovation	12,133	-0.11	1.03	–	–	ns
Dynamism	12,133	0.11	0.94	–	–	ns
Work	12,133	-0.04	0.56	–	–	ns
Hobbies	12,133	0.12	0.59	–	–	ns
Proactiveness	12,133	0.17	0.55	–	–	ns
Markets	12,133	-0.09	0.54	–	–	ns
Technocratization	12,133	0.04	0.17	–	–	ns
Paperwork	12,133	0.01	0.05	–	–	ns

Df=Degree of Freedom; B=Standardized regression weights; T=T Ratio; R=Multiple Correlation; P=Level of Significance.

It appears that the meaningful predictors for the profit-making group are the differentiation aspect of structure and heterogeneity in environment. The meaningful predictors for the loss-making group are the time spent on social life, meetings, work overload, and the technocratization aspect of structure. The differentiation aspect of structure is useful for the profit-making group, and the employment of scientists and technologists is useful for the loss-making group.

The aspects of strategy-making, the environment and structure can explain 18 per cent of variance for the internals and eight per cent for the externals. For internals, the futurity and proactivity strategies, and the technocratization aspect of structure have positive value, while the risk-taking strategy has negative weight. For the externals, proactivity, risk-taking and innovation strategies, and the technocratization and differentiation aspects of structure are positive predictors.

Table 8.5: Regression Analysis for Loss-Making Corporations.
Dependent Variable: Professional Commitment

Predictors	Df	B	T	R	R^2	P
Social life	13,107	0.96	3.20	0.65	0.42	0.01
Technocratization	13,107	0.83	2.08	–	–	0.05
Work overload	13,107	0.76	1.97	–	–	0.10
Meetings	13,107	0.62	1.87	–	–	0.10
Paperwork	13,107	0.38	1.50	–	–	ns
Risk-taking	13,107	0.19	1.31	–	–	ns
Heterogeneity	13,107	0.08	0.82	–	–	ns
Work	13,107	-0.18	0.82	–	–	ns
Markets	13,107	0.43	0.97	–	–	ns
Futurity	13,107	0.07	1.13	–	–	ns
Internality–Externality	13,107	0.14	1.15	–	–	ns
Dynamism	13,107	0.04	0.54	–	–	ns
Scanning	13,107	-0.04	0.43	–	–	ns
Differentiation	13,107	0.03	0.35	–	–	ns

Df=Degree of Freedom; B=Standardized regression weights; T=T Ratio; R=Multiple Correlation; P=Level of Significance.

The maximum variance explained in the internality-oriented group (39 per cent) is higher than in the externality-oriented group (28 per cent) (Tables 8.6 and 8.7). The spending of time on social life and on meetings, the number of technically qualified persons employed and the use of the futurity and risk-taking strategies are good predictors for the internality-oriented managers. The extra time spent on work, differentiated structures, time on meetings, paperwork and social life predict the professional commitment of the externality-oriented managers.

Table 8.6: Regression Analysis for Internality-Oriented Managers.
Dependent Variable: Professional Commitment

Predictors	Df	B	T	R	R^2	P
Social life	16,111	1.10	2.46	0.62	0.39	0.01
Risk-taking	16,111	0.93	2.42	–	–	0.01
Technocratization	16,111	0.68	1.81	–	–	0.10
Futurity	16,111	0.61	1.78	–	–	0.10
Meetings	16,111	0.51	1.72	–	–	0.10
Heterogeneity	16,111	0.40	1.22	–	–	ns
Work overload	16,111	0.36	1.09	–	–	ns
Hobbies	16,111	0.36	1.15	–	–	ns
Work	16,111	0.25	0.75	–	–	ns
Dynamism	16,111	0.06	0.81	–	–	ns
Paperwork	16,111	0.13	0.65	–	–	ns
Differentiation	16,111	0.05	0.49	–	–	ns
Planning and managing	16,111	-0.07	0.30	–	–	ns
Innovation	16,111	-0.02	0.21	–	–	ns
Market	16,111	0.07	0.19	–	–	ns
Scanning	16,111	-0.01	0.11	–	–	ns
Proactivity	16,111	0.02	0.10	–	–	ns

Df=Degree of Freedom; B=Standardized regression weights; T=T Ratio; R=Multiple Correlation; P=Level of Significance.

Table 8.7: Regression Analysis for Externality-Oriented Managers.
Dependent Variable: Professional Commitment

Predictors	Df	B	T	R	R^2	P
Work overload	16,123	1.05	2.94	0.53	0.28	0.01
Meetings	16,123	1.01	2.65	–	–	0.01
Paperwork	16,123	0.78	2.13	–	–	0.05
Differentiation	16,123	0.62	2.11	–	–	0.05
Social life	16,123	0.57	1.72	–	–	0.10
Technocratization	16,123	0.38	1.26	–	–	ns
Heterogeneity	16,123	0.29	0.99	–	–	ns
Planning and managing	16,123	0.20	0.89	–	–	ns
Scanning	16,123	-0.11	1.30	–	–	ns
Innovation	16,123	0.13	1.08	–	–	ns
Futurity	16,123	0.04	0.74	–	–	ns
Risk-taking	16,123	-0.11	0.76	–	–	ns
Dynamism	16,123	-0.03	0.36	–	–	ns
Work	16,123	-0.06	0.26	–	–	ns
Markets	16,123	-0.10	0.25	–	–	ns
Proactivity	16,123	0.02	0.15	–	–	ns
Hobbies	16,123	0.04	0.12	–	–	ns

Df=Degree of Freedom; B=Standardized regression weights; T=T Ratio; R=Multiple Correlation; P=Level of Significance.

In all the cases, the higher the professional commitment, the higher are the achieved goals, the clearly perceived roles and the higher confidence in the presence of turbulent and uncertain business environment. The fact that professional commitment is equally high in the two sectors reflects the use of comparable recruitment and selection policies in the two sectors. Both equally emphasize the need for well-prepared and professionally qualified manpower. There may also be similar emphasis on training and on attending professional courses and conferences so that one can bring renewed vigour to the job. The emphasis is thus on competency-based management. Holland (1986) has talked of competency-based management and observed that managers may need five types of competencies:

1. Cognitive competencies help managers to build up their potential as a team, process relevant information and be critically involved in the quality of planning, organizing and decision-making.
2. Motivational competencies provide managers with skills to motivate others, and are important in improving the quality of products or services of communication and work life.
3. Leadership competencies are important in bringing the clarity of purpose to the people in the organization, and in building visions, values and cultural identity.
4. Achievement competencies provide a foundation to the manager's potential to achieve goals.
5. Job functions include organizational sensitivity, management control, organizational ability and delegation.

Most managers who are seniors and near the top of the hierarchy need all the types of the competencies at one time or the other. The typical competencies in which outstanding managers distinguish themselves include conceptualization of the problem and synthetic thinking, and planning and causal thinking that guide the resolution of conflicts (Klemp and McClelland, 1986). Managers need both formal and tacit knowledge. The tacit knowledge can help them in managing self, managing tasks and managing others (Wagner and Sternberg, 1986). Statistically significant associations have been reported by Willer and Henderson (1988) between the communication competency of managers and employees' satisfaction, their sense of role clarity, perceptions of supervisors' effectiveness and perceptions of their work unit's effectiveness.

Summary

The analysis reveals that there are no significant differences in the managerial profiles of the public versus private sectors, profit-making versus loss-making groups and internality- versus externality-oriented managers on professional commitment. Some differences in relationships are seen with the aspects of time management, indicating the effects of context and the nature of corporations. In all the cases, the correlations with goal achievement, role perceptions and confidence are positive. The risk-taking strategy is important for the profit-making and internality-oriented groups. The proactivity strategy is useful for the private sector and internality- as well as externality-oriented managers. The futurity strategy is important for all professionally committed managers. The differentiation aspect of structure is relevant to the public sector, the profit-making corporations, and the externality-oriented group. The variables of time management, strategy, environment, structure and personal orientation explain the professional commitment of managers in the private sector (65 per cent) better than in the public sector (27 per cent). The prediction is also better for the loss-making group (42 per cent) and for the internality-oriented group (39 per cent) than for the profit-making group (24 per cent) and for the externality-oriented managers (28 per cent).

9

SOME MORE GLEANINGS

Qualitative Data

Additional insight into corporate functioning came from the process and contents of the semi-structured interviews-cum-discussions with the managers, observations and records of critical events. These have been separately analyzed to identify the dominant issues underlying the management practices. They have also been compared and then pooled together to yield an integrated view. The number of respondents interviewed has been smaller than the number of those who filled the questionnaires. Some respondents participated in the detailed discussions and accepted the questionnaire, but did not return the completed questionnaire to us even after repeated requests and appointments. A small number of respondents in fact even said that they had mailed the completed questionnaires, but they may not have reached us. Then there were some who completed the questionnaire, but excused themselves from discussion under some pretense or the other. Some went on to comment that they had already invested much of their time and effort in filling the questionnaire and that we should feel happy and fortunate.

The discussions encompass a wide range of issues: the perceived order in their offices, the years spent in the corporations, their roles, their views on the public sector and the private sector, industrial policy, labour legislation, capacity utilization, the role of chairman/managing director in the corporation, government interventions (policy specific and operational), constraints and future challenges. The observational records include behavioural reactions of managers to the points raised or implied, the type of behaviour displayed towards different employees and visitors, encounters, comments and suggestions etc. A few critical incidents that just happened in the presence of the research team, like the news circulated about the appointment of a new chairman in one corporation, the handling of a junior employee who did not do what he had been asked to do by the senior manager, and the reactions of a senior manager when his personal assistant told the researcher that the boss was away from the office even though he was very much in the office, have also been analyzed and integrated with the rest of the data.

The content analysis procedures have been used to evolve the categories, and to club together and label the diverse expressions and statements. Each interview has been read by a minimum of two and maximum of three persons and an agreement reached about the major and minor themes. The interviews have been analyzed for the themes explicit or/and implicit, and then the major dimensions have been formulated. Data have been summarized in the form of the frequency distributions of responses. The response analyses in terms of percentages are presented for the public and private sectors in Table 9.1, and for the profit- and loss-making public sector corporations in Table 9.2.

Highlights

General

Respondents unanimously agree that the public sector is the mainstay of the five-year plans. What the corporations are expected to contribute to the national economy should thus be reflected in their performance, capacity utilization, achievement of socio-political objectives, profitability etc. Corporate goals are specified on the basis of the political and economic agenda, and the senior managers are expected to formulate and undertake action plans to achieve them by using the systems and procedures, the resources and the technology available in the industrial environment. A greater clarity of goals, the use of appropriate techniques, adequate preparation and the drawing of contingency plans on the part of the managers

Table 9.1: Summary of Content Analysis of Interview Responses
for Public and Private Sectors

Dimension		Public N=146	Private N=40
		in per cent	
Team spirit	High	48	65
	Moderate	32	25
	Low	20	10
Topmen's perception	Authoritarian	28	50
	Consultative	43	20
	Acceptable	17	30
	Powerless	12	–
Policies	Efficient	42	75
	Inefficient	22	15
	Uncertain	36	10
Decision-making	Topmen	25	68
	Government	25	6
	Joint	25	15
	Employees	25	10
Manager–Employee relations	Proper	68	50
	Doubtful	26	25
	Lacking	6	25
Planning process	Productive	40	70
	Wasteful	40	5
	Doubtful	20	25
Work process	Efficient	40	75
	Inefficient	28	15
	Degenerative	32	10
Future perceptions of output	High Cost	35	40
	Normal	43	50
	Loss-making	22	10

are essential for all-round corporate growth.

The public sector has multiple goals, and yet in reality no corporation pursues any goal in an unambiguous manner. In fact, there has been no one goal in any corporation that can be clearly pinpointed as the goal pursued by the managers at different levels. The contradictions in goals and priorities at the corporate level have transcended the roles of the seniormost managers and the policies

Table 9.2: Summary of Content Analysis of Interview Responses for Profit- and Loss-Making Corporations in the Public Sector

Dimension		Profit-Making N=81	Loss-Making N=65
		in per cent	
Team spirit	High	66	30
	Moderate	29	35
	Low	5	35
Topmen's perception	Authoritarian	26	30
	Consultative	56	30
	Acceptable	19	14
	Powerless	8	16
Policies	Efficient	48	35
	Inefficient	20	25
	Uncertain	32	40
Decision-making	Topmen	30	20
	Government	40	20
	Joint	42	10
	Employees	20	30
Manager–Employee relations	Proper	75	60
	Doubtful	22	30
	Lacking	3	10
Planning process	Productive	40	20
	Wasteful	40	40
	Doubtful	20	20
Work process	Efficient	55	25
	Inefficient	5	50
	Degenerative	20	25
Future perceptions of output	High cost	20	50
	Normal	60	25
	Loss-making	20	25
Personnel Policy	Self Development	80	25
	Helpful	10	40
	Lack policy	5	25
	Unfocused	5	10

adopted by corporations. Managers are uncertain about their expected role behaviour and actions. They are often ambivalent in their attitudes. They tend to search for job definitions and meanings in the notes and writings of the concerned ministries and other documents, and thus often make wrong or incomplete decisions.

All corporations do not have the same history of development.

Some of the corporations have been established in the post-Independence period, some have been reorganized to fit new descriptions by converting government departments and sick units. While in the former type the good and bad procedures and practices have taken shape during their life-time operations and have not been imported from the other organizations, the latter type have invariably inherited the problems as well as the culture of the earlier units, and continue to have them. The attempts to get rid of the failures of the past have not been really successful.

The autonomy of the public sector is found to be a myth. The search for new challenges, the acceptance of different ideas, plans, and the value of achievement and growth does not prevail in many of the public sector enterprises. Planning is an important corporate activity to be undertaken on a regular basis, but it is not given adequate attention even in the best functioning and profit-generating units. The planning process is made deliberately cumbersome, inflexible and unrealistic, and it fails to reflect the goals of planned growth, efficiency and profitability. No manager feels like taking time-bound planning exercises and project implementation jobs seriously. There are, however, some sectoral differences. The flawed planning and poor work culture result in inadequate capacity utilization in a larger number of public enterprises than in private sector enterprises. Nearly 40 per cent of the managers in the public sector find the planning process wasteful as compared with the 5 per cent in the private sector. The situation has not been different between the profit- and the loss-making corporations.

Time management happens to be the greatest casualty in the public sector, although it ought to be considered vital to the efficiency and effectiveness of all enterprises. The prohibitive controls from above and the unproductive work culture within have made the concept of time in the cognition of employees redundant. A vicious circle is in operation in which inadequate allocation of resources leads to the choice of inferior technology, lower time inputs, lower production, lower capacity utilization, lower resource generation and so on. The inflexible, lengthy and cumbersome systems and procedures add fuel to the fire and lead to cost overruns, huge losses and deflated employee morale. The systems and procedures for filing, accounting, contracting and marketing need to be updated and computerized in order to free the employees' time and divert it away from the unproductive work practices. The corporate norms should be evolved to put the pressure on employees to undertake useful activities in an expeditious manner and thereby help the corporations to achieve functional efficiency of a high order.

Institution-building requires the evolving and perusal of sound policies, adequate resource-generation and mobilization, development of better professional and human skills in employees and overall a professional management. It is not found possible by managers in public sector corporations because of the contradictory objectives adopted by them. In fact the anomalies have been commonly used to shield inaction at every level. The misuse of resources has been intense so as to provoke many to comment that the public sector is treated like a community cow which can be milked by any one who can get away with it. Managers symbolize indeed a sort of split personality, where they resent instructions from above and yet they do not act without them. They like the juniors to respect them but fail to show any respect themselves.

Communication skills are important managerial skills as well as a provision in effective organizations, but management as well as employees lack these skills. Most managers lack the conviction that communication is important and do not try to master the necessary skills. They find it psychologically difficult to accept that they are part of the same corporate network as the juniors and thus they practise selective and incomplete communication. Employees have a tendency to distort it further and colour it in terms of their own experiences, motivations and choices. In the atmosphere of distrust that prevails, everyone suffers and the corporation suffers the most.

The social system is collectivity-oriented and reinforces inter-dependence in relationships, caring for each other, family and personal affinities, and employees invariably look at corporations as mini-social systems. The employees desire to develop community feelings at work and be treated with sympathy and a personal touch. They undermine the importance of individual responsibility and commit-ment to work and the organization.

In the present group, a substantially higher percentage of managers in the public sector (68 per cent) see the management–employee relations as proper against 50 per cent in the private sector. Thus, while the hierarchical distance seems to be larger in the private sector, the manager–employee relations need to be improved sub-stantially in both. The good interpersonal relations and positive work climate may be used as incentives. A balance between individual and group-based expectations and responsibility is desirable, towards which managers as well as others should work. It is more so because the money is no longer seen as a motivation by employees in the organized setting and particularly in the public sector. It is advocated for the benefit of those who have good interpersonal relations that the contribution of individuals ought to be recognized and those in need should be helped through management development and counselling programmes.

Policies of Government

The government policies of licensing, manufacturing, technology regulation, pricing, costing, marketing and labour have been designed by focusing on the public sector. Most public sector corporations operate under monopolistic or highly protracted conditions. While they have been able to sell even sub-standard goods at their own terms and price, the employees have not only not learnt, but they refuse to learn to operate under competitive market conditions. They do not find themselves able to use any type of competitive advantage. In industries like drugs, cement and textiles, whenever the government policy has shifted towards decontrol, even the well-functioning corporations have run into losses. The necessary readjustments have not been made. The attempt has been to let the corporations lose and then let the government revert the policies. The private sector has adopted relatively more modern and efficient technology, and have developed a work culture in which individual managers have responsibility to a large extent. Not only do they succeed in breaking even, but they also earn profits. They have clearer goals and a commercial motto which enables them to use it to their competitive advantage.

Managerial efficiency and competency are not considered to be really important in the public sector, and are not fostered in the true sense. If some corporations are doing well and generating profits, it is not because the managers in some corporations are more competent, but because they have the advantage of the pricing policy of the government, favourable rules and regulations, and protective laws. The wage policy of the government is lopsided, and adversely affects the negotiations and wage settlements. As a policy, no public sector corporations have been closed down even after recurring heavy losses year after year. Management as well as employees have exploited it to their advantage. Some private sector enterprises have been forced to make an exit.

Most managers feel that some reforms in labour legislation are necessary to improve the industrial environment in the country and to introduce professionalism in business operations. The prevalent tendency of normless unionization among employees and the existence of multiple unions under the umbrella of various political parties is cutting deeply into the roots of the corporate bodies. The percentage of managers who perceive the present policy to be efficient has been much less in the public sector (42 per cent) than in the private sector (75 per cent). In the public sector, the profit-making corporations are marginally in a better position than the loss-making corporations.

The policy changes have been made not because of the productive needs of the industry, but under pressure from the various power groups, be it the industry itself, landowners, the union or the changed political perceptions. Frequently the policies are vague, non-directional and incongruent with other policy prescriptions. The recruitment policies in the public sector are positively biased towards the average performer and the non-performers in the name of equity and social justice.

Most managers (82 per cent), irrespective of the sector, felt dissatisfied with the policy of reservations in employment and promotion. The way it is implemented indicates that the policy is not in the interest of the corporate sector. Reservation should be confined to the stage of initial recruitment. The policy of promotion should not differentiate between Scheduled Caste/Scheduled Tribe and non-Scheduled Caste/non-Scheduled Tribe. Once given the opportunity to learn on the job, all employees should make conscious efforts to prove their worth. The rich and the advantaged among the SC/ST (those who have had the advantage of good educational institutions) should not be given any special entitlements. They can be given additional monetary benefits and other supportive facilities to develop themselves, but competence should not be compromised. Non-recognition of merit while on the job has a negative impact on the work climate. Given the present political scenario, the situation may not change towards the better in the future. Then there are other distorted realities. There are employees (schemers) with ministerial connections waiting in the wings, for whom the chiefs ignore all the principles of fairplay. The common and competent recruit is made to feel small and incompetent. Such policies and practices are necessarily dys-functional in the short run, and would weaken the organizational fabric in the long run.

The policies of licensing and regulating have proved counter-productive. While delays in licensing etc. are endemic to the public and the private sectors, the latter is even more at the mercy of the bureaucracy. It often takes about 3-8 months for an industrialist to obtain a letter of intent from the ministry for a project, 4-6 months to convert it into a license, and 6-12 months for the clearance from the Monopolies and Restrictive Trade Practices Commission (MRTPC) and the Company Law Board. It should be realized that the loss of time means loss of the money as well. The government should change its policy of functioning as parallel task masters to the corporations. The corporations should be allowed to function within the broad national policy framework.

The policies are not seen as instruments of improving the status quo. The lack of clear governmental policies makes their translation into possible contingency plans of action difficult. A higher per cent of managers in the public sector (75 per cent) observed that even the existing policies can be used efficiently, if the political bosses left them alone. Distortions in policies are compounded because of the external controls.

Environment

The external environment is seen as one that is quite turbulent because of policy contradictions, insufficient freedom of action and resources. The resources are under pressure from within and outside, having roots in the corporations' multiple objectives, labour legislation, unions, interference from ministries and inter-ministry rivalries. There are also pressures from international agencies. There is need to identify new markets and new technological innovations to be able to generate profits and to earn foreign exchange which is making extra demands on resources, which are not met ever.

The political climate in the country is exploitative, uncertain and emotionally surcharged; a climate in which keeping the labour quiet is valued. Labour unions strive to keep themselves in power by keeping their pressure on the management for higher wages in the form of tactics rather than talk about work, quality control etc., while the management waits for inter-union rivalry to continue and thereby escape/delay decision-making. It is only in the last few years that some corporations have adopted the policy of signing a Memorandum of Understanding (MoU) with the unions. A substantial percentage of the manager's time gets consumed in negotiating with unions on issues that are trivial. The aim is to tire out one or the other, and the consequence is a win-lose situation. The continued struggle with the rival politically linked labour unions has made the managements increasingly weak, and the industrial climate of the country fragile. Good management needs both adaptability and accommodation, as they are required to pursue proactivity and futurity strategies, to face environmental challenges and read the signals with promptness, and on a continued basis to be able to react in an appropriate manner. They need good scanning, forecasting and monitoring techniques at their disposal and the freedom of action.

Ineffectiveness of Boards

Theoretically, management boards or boards of directors are an essential organ in the corporate system as they serve important functions. According to Drucker (1976), boards are expected to discharge six functions:

1. Boards can help the corporation to ensure strong competent management on a continued basis;
2. Boards can make management focus on crucial questions;
3. Boards can act as the conscience of the corporation and can act independently with strength and conviction;
4. Board members can be the confidants of the top-level managers and share their doubts and uncertainties;
5. Boards can provide windows to the outside world; and
6. Boards can be more credible to the public.

The board of directors has the overall responsibility for corporate management. It should lay down the policy, take important decisions and accept responsibility for the performance of the corporation, although in practice it is no more than a 'rubber stamping' authority. It is felt that different corporate bodies demand different perspectives and management, and this should be reflected in the constitution of boards. The members would need to present different mixes of planning, organizing, staffing, motivating, controlling and directing in different corporate contexts. For instance, the production-oriented industry cannot be equated with the service-oriented industry. A loss-making and sick industry cannot be equated with a profit-making and growing industry.

Boards are ineffective as of now. They fail to exercise any control on the functioning of corporations. In fact, the inefficiencies are now seen as inbuilt aspects of the constitution of the Board. The members of the board are nominated on the basis of their connections with the political bosses, rather than for their competence or interest in the management of corporations. One member is often a member of several other boards of the corporations (10-15). Many of them do not read the agenda and the relevant papers circulated to them well in advance. They come to the meetings, if they come at all, preoccupied with some other concerns. The discussions are kept limited to the agenda and do not last for more than 45 minutes or an hour at the most. They do not spend time on thinking/discussing the problems of any one corporation. Their interests are often confined to minor perks like guest houses and transport. If the board members are conscious of their obligations and responsibilities, they should not accept the memberships of so many corporations and they should demand accountability of the top-level managers and the executive team. Decisions are often taken by the political bosses and the chairmen a priori and boards are used to legitimize them. The boards are not able to do things right, nor are they able to do the right things.

In fact, in both the public and private sectors, the boards have become increasingly ineffective. A high percentage of managers (77.5 per cent) perceive this to be a direct consequence of the enhanced powers of the chief executives. It is felt that effectiveness of the board can be restored by changing the attitudes of the government and the owners. Most managers feel that in its present form the board is really not necessary. It is in general either unwilling or unable to contribute to the strategic decisions of corporations. Often, the members play contradictory and dubious roles, giving an impression that the purpose is to restrain the operations of management, rather than to promote efficiency. It is desired, however, that the board should be seen as provider and facilitator of the corporate vision, and not as one placed opposite to management.

Corporate Culture

The culture of a corporation reflects the system of public and collective operation and the accepted meanings of the given reality for a given group at a given time. It includes symbols, ideologies, beliefs, rituals, myths, norms and behavioural expectations. According to Schall (1983) these are the shared realities which contribute to the uniqueness of behaviour expectations. Goodstein (1983) has expressed the view that organizations, like persons, have values; and these values are integrated into some coherent value system. In any organization, the members generally have a set of beliefs about what is appropriate and inappropriate organizational behaviour. It is also referred to as frames of meaning (Spybey, 1984).

The public sector corporations are microcosms of the larger social systems and reflect the socio-political culture of the country in which there is little effort on development. There are inadequacies in the managerial culture, styles, systems and skills. There is no specific identity of different corporations. There are no common purposes and shared values among the people at the top, meaning that there are no agreed visions of the future. There is a high degree of politicization as all corporations are controlled by one ministry or the other, and there has been almost an 'obsession with controls'. There are endless incipient ego clashes at all levels that are almost pathological in loss-making corporations. There are always some actors who are winners and some who are losers, but what has not been recognized is the fact that in the process the greatest losers have been the corporations themselves. Within each corporation there are deep-rooted cliques and alliances and these surface more in the loss-making corporations, where the cliques become critical as they tend to gang up against their own colleagues.

The prevalent corporate culture is characterized by conflicting demands and expectations of groups and members at each level. Members as individuals are interested in deriving optimum benefits out of their corporate membership and make only a minimal required contribution. At the highest level, the chairmen/ managing directors are interested in keeping their positions protected from the political bosses as well as the threats and criticisms of labour unions, as both can be expensive. At the lower level, the protection is sought against the actions of corporate bosses and workers, but at the highest level, the goal is confined to managing the corporate show in some way or the other so as to maintain the status quo. How it is being done or/and what are the likely long-term repercussions of such a myopic approach for corporate functioning have obviously little relevance. The directors get conflicting signals from their bosses (chairmen/ managing directors), and little positive feedback from their subordinates. The situation becomes still more ambiguous and confusing at the level of general manager, deputy general managers etc. The managements' concern and concentration are diverted away from profitability, technology upgradation and resource mobilization to trivial issues of receiving visitors, arranging functions and listening to the subordinate employees. While the job obligations include equal number of 'dos' and 'don'ts', the managers have to focus on 'don'ts' mostly. There is a high premium on keeping the political bosses and bureaucrats in the ministry in good spirits than the work commitment.

Theoretically, all political bosses and corporate chiefs clamour about pursuing the professional approach in management, but in practice the same persons set it aside because it does not suit either the political bosses or the subordinate employees. The work climate is not receptive for any systematic managerial approach. It has been a widely shared perception of the senior managers that the corporate culture in the public sector is maintenance-oriented, rather than growth- or production- oriented. The focus is on structural aspects, routine, rules and procedures. The bureaucracy is advocated and practised with heart and soul in it and condemned at the same time. Since most corporations have the government model of bureaucracy implanted in them, they have a heavy administrative infrastructure, committees and paperwork, and complete insensitivity to the needs of the industry and to the purpose of the origin of corporate sector. In fact, more often than not, the bureaucratic set-up comes in the way like an insurmountable rock and by the time one manages to cross it, one finds that the decision has lost its relevance and thus an opportunity. The public sector set-up truly represents an inflexible configuration (what Mintzberg (1979) has described as 'machine bureaucracy') which is built only for one purpose. It is efficient in its own limited domain, but cannot easily adapt itself to another domain. Above all, it refuses to tolerate an environment that may be heterogeneous, dynamic and changing.

The bureaucratic set-up has made cadre and promotions based on seniority deep-rooted concepts in the corporations. The career progression path can pass only within the same cadre. Horizontal movement can be possible only at the initial recruitment stage. A crossing over afterwards leads to a violent hue and cry in general. The policy of promotion in the management cadre is more personalized in the private sector, as it represents a mix of owner control and professionalism, even if it utilizes these concepts to earn optimum profits.

In the public sector there are contrasting pulls in all directions. There is a high degree of inertia in the structures and resistance among the people to do even the routine prescribed jobs honestly, let alone the extra ones. There are umpteen instances of heavy compromises, inefficiencies, fudged responsibility and wastage on the public exchequer, but really without any concern. As some managers observe in some corporations the situation is a 'free-for-all'. There are heterogeneous job demands, less documentation of jobs and too many restrictions/checks on allowing people to work. Little constructive dialogue takes place even among the seniors. There are numerous meetings, but few decisions; numerous groups, but few teams. Routine work and paperwork have become substitutes for thinking. A higher team-spirit has been reported in the private sector (65 per cent) than in the public sector (48 per cent). Only 10 per cent managers in the private sector have reported poor team-spirit against 20 per cent in the public sector. Within the public sector, profit-making corporations have higher team-spirit than loss-making corporations.

An adhoc approach characterizes the corporate operations. There is no long-term planning. There is no authentic system of performance appraisal. Being non-productive is the norm. A lot of effort and time are consumed in religiously pursuing the existing systems and procedures. The general work culture is one of no urgency, least involvement and complete apathy. Populism and sychophancy are visibly advocated as most chairmen want peace during their tenure. There are interpersonal jealousies among managers. The personal and work ethics are not of a high order. Some have highly cynical attitudes. They fail to see themselves playing any constructive roles. Some of them feel though that the development of the right type of attitudes is necessary. Personal involvement in the job, imagination, perspective and coordination are the necessary managerial skills.

The fact that most public sectors have operated so far like monopolies has made them feel that there are virtually no competitors.

The special position of the public sector has inculcated a peculiar kind of psychology among the employees at all levels; they feel that they are special people who can get special treatment on demand. The chairmen and senior managers do not initiate any negative action as it may reflect on them negatively, and the government does not take any negative action because of the fear of losing popularity. In the private sector the work culture is more manager-focused than government-oriented. Managers have the legitimate position and power to act, if they decide to do so.

There is discord and lack of coordination in planning and responsibility at the highest level of operation. Coordination seems to be the greatest casualty of the public sector. Sometimes one corporation is managed by three ministries, and thus it tends to receive three different advices on the same issues. Sometimes a corporation is under one ministry, but the ministry gives ambiguous and multiple advices. Good coordination is necessary among the various agencies related to a public sector corporation, such as ministries, government departments etc.. It has been the shared perception of managers at all levels that the ministries should lay down general guidelines, and then let the corporations have full responsibility to implement them. The difficulties also arise because the workers' expectations are in conflict with the expectations of the government. The management has to bear the brunt of this incongruence.

Inadequate communication and feedback systems have generated misperceptions, distrust and tensions at all levels. Regardless of what the management may do, even their positive decisions are suspected as being part of some conspiracy, and they are resisted by causing disruptions of numerous types in the functioning. There is little trust between managers and workers. Employees only expect positive action, and increasing returns. Either they do not understand the reality or they deliberately ignore it. Management can do hundreds of good things for the employees, but one refusal or necessary negative action tends to destroy all the goodwill. The trust between managers and workers is not there.

Top Leadership

In the socio-cultural context of the country, the personality cult has been an important aspect of organizational functioning, and continues to be so in the public sector as well as in the private sector. This brings into focus the chief executive officers in the corporation, whose vision, commitment, involvement, ability to influence different components in the environment, clarity and decision-making are important. This requires them to be persons who would match the importance of the job given to them. While in most private sector corporations, the owner/chairman of the board likes to hire a known person or a close relative, in most public sector corporations this does not happen. More often than not the appointed chairmen are not the men who deserve the post. Political preference and acceptability, rather than their merit and competence, form important considerations. The process of appointment of the chairmen is made an unduly complex and long-drawn affair. It has been observed that the file of a chief executive officer/managing director has to 'pass through' nearly 17 desks before he gets the orders. There are quite a few corporations at any one point of time which may not have the chiefs in position and operate under the ad hoc/acting head in a casual manner.

In both public and private sectors, the chief executives' jobs are insecure in one way or the other. In the public sector the chief executives are expected to go along with the political bosses, while in the private sector they must live up to the owners' expectations. A chief executive officer can be removed on a trivial pretext, as and when the government wishes. In fact, this strategy has been used by the government to disguise poor corporate performance in the public sector. This invariably haunts the successors and leads to their subsequent failure. Competent leadership is resisted even within the corporate body through the tactics of non-compliance and passive resistance. Indecisiveness characterizes the chief executive officers and creates an atmosphere of casualness at all levels. The quality of leadership is not always high. They talk, write notes, form committees, make lengthy plans, but avoid coming to decisions, until they get a clear signal to do so from the government. Decision-making at the top and seniormost levels reflects a high degree of ambivalence, a 'wait and watch' approach as the occupants of these positions are not secure in their saddles. Informed decision-making in an integrated manner is necessary, but it is not practised.

Chief executives are expected to identify the corporate goals clearly, prioritize and pursue them with freedom of action. They need to concretize the abstract goals, so that the managers at the middle and lower levels can have a clear agenda for action. The chiefs set the tone of the organizational culture. They have the responsibility of creating a climate of trust, respect and acceptance. Their sensitivities to the needs and expectations of the people, situations and tasks are important. They have to have a commercial motto, together with vision and luck. They have to act as agents of authority and prophets of organizational development at the same time. Some risk-taking on the part of chief executive officers is necessary and important. They ought to initiate timely action otherwise they would set inertia and lose their image.

It is believed that one's sincerity mirrors through one's actions, and the chiefs are no exception. If one functions in a clandestine manner, one would meet sooner or later appropriate resistance at all stages. A good chairman must face squarely the differences with employees at different levels; he must understand, analyze, explain and put an end to the practice of compromises. He should develop organizational norms that would encompass value commitment, performance and positive actions.

Human relations are important and basic to corporate survival and growth, in which the senior managers are at the centrestage. It has been felt by many managers that the chairmen/managing directors should have genuine concern for all employees. There must be some personal touch even in formal systems. An employee's personal qualities rather than his/her file should be the basis of decision-making. This also seems congruent to the observation that in Indian organizations most employees are bound by the oath of loyalty. This loyalty is, in practice, towards a particular person. It is important and meaningful for employees to identify with whom they work, rather than with a faceless and impersonal work system. Loyalty has earned premiums for employees, either in terms of over-time payments or other schemes. Day-to-day interference from the government and ministry have eroded the authority of chiefs and has caused increased dependencies and helplessness. This ought to be contained.

The percentage of managers who reported that the top-level managers in their corporations acted by consultation is not comparable in the private (20 per cent) and the public (43 per cent) sectors. A higher percentage (50 per cent) in the private sector found them authoritative. This is understandable in view of the direct control of the corporations by their owners in the private sector. Within the public sector, a higher percentage in the profit-making corporations have reported that the chairmen/managing directors were of a consultative type (56 per cent), as compared with the loss-making corporations (30 per cent). Only 4 per cent managers in the loss-making corporations, than the profit-making corporations perceive the chairmen/managing directors as authoritative. Some are not able to categorize the chiefs into consultative or authoritative types. Their roles are found mixed.

A good deal of indifference, skepticism and helplessness characterizes the attitudes of the top-level and seniormost managers in the public sector. Many of them have high professional qualifications and sophisticated training and are expected to have a professional approach in their dealings. It is not found true in practice, however. They do not identify with the corporation in the real sense, and often show a casual and half-hearted approach. A larger number grumble about one type of facility or the other even in the profit-making corporations. It seems a far cry to have a professional managerial culture implanted in Indian industry. Such a culture is not valued in the society, or in the corporate sector. There is an undue aura attached to the positions, and to obtain them all accepted procedures are undermined.

It is desired that the role of managers in all corporations should be facilitative and educative rather than controlling. A management style is desired that would fit the cultural ethos of employees and the society. The managers who adopt the role of benevolent fathers are found relatively more successful. It has been argued that a good management should worry about the entire family of the employee and not the employee alone, as the norm in the society is one of interdependence between the family and the work life of employees. While many senior executives found policy ambiguity an obstacle, an equal number found it an advantage/asset. While the former feel that an unambiguous policy can be used to mobilize political opposition against them by the powers that be, as and when considered convenient, the latter think that it gives them a handle to interpret it as they feel appropriate in their situation. They find it safe to avoid being deeply immersed in policy details.

The pressure to bridge the competing demands of different groups reduces the management function to marginality. They are expected to cope with confrontation without being confrontational, have good political skills and not be politicized, develop good working relationships and yet maintain a distance, and create a feeling among the opposing groups that they are treated fairly, even when they are not. Further, political bosses keep changing and managers have a tremendous responsibility of minimizing discontinuities in corporate operations and thus the stress. It has been advocated that senior managers should learn the skill of managing the policy agenda, take into account even events that may be peripheral to the corporations, and skilfully use standard operating procedures as control mechanisms.

What managers perceive as the desired qualities of a good chief executive officer be specified as below:

1. Clear vision;
2. Clear delegation of authority;
3. Direction and overall supervision;
4. Responsible and supportive behaviour;
5. Ability to enjoy the trust of the people at all levels in the organization;
6. Encouragement of the growth and development of subordinates; and
7. Good public relations.

Reward Power

Managers have too often complained that they are not given the authority commensurate with responsibility. The lack of incentives and the reward power of executives in the public sector have made them powerless. The official provisions include some degree of coercive power like memos, warnings etc., which only tend to aggravate the problem, given the prevalent labour legislation, political climate and the attitude of unions. The disciplinary process has been made unduly lengthy, complex and unrealistic by labour legislation and redundant by the political bosses. All managers prefer not to be involved in any litigation. Superiors do not feel that they have enough conviction and the courage to take disciplinary action against their erring subordinates. This has made the organizations anarchical. The managers are more than aware that standing up for a principle would mean the stoppage of work and their shouldering of additional responsibility for the work. They can be publicly mauled by the government, humiliated and assaulted by the union members, their families can be harassed, and then they can be transferred and/or made to resign. Most labour legislation favours the workers. The systems of using the confidential reports of employees as the instrument of discipline has become obsolete and meaningless. The system still insists on these reports, ignoring that it takes time and generates unpleasantness. Some managers feel that these reports are used so circuitously now that rewards are not given, but punishment is not forgotten.

The situation in the private sector is somewhat more flexible. The managers still have the power of 'hire and fire' practised in a very subtle way. Profits are important for everyone and at all levels. Also, the top-level managers of private companies are under the direct supervision of the owners, and subject to reinforcements.

Participation in Decision-making

The practice of participative decision-making is instituted in all corporations, but it is more successful in some corporations than in others. Even in the corporations significantly manned by professionals the participation does not include decision-making at all levels and with equal commitment. In some corporations and that too at some levels, it has been used as a tool to reach more informed and shared decisions, while in some corporations it has been used as an opportunity to air their grievances.

Delegation of authority has not been clear. It is inadequate and grossly faulty. The delegation of power is nominal in some and average in others, but not ideal in any corporation. Delegation is more clear-cut, even if it is limited in the private sector. Also, not all managers display equal competence in the use of authority, which varies from person to person and from situation to situation. Even if there is substantial delegation, some people do not have the psychological make-up to use it. They always pass the responsibility to their seniors.

The provision of participative decision-making in most public sector corporations extends from shop-floor upwards, but it remains so only on paper. Meetings are infrequent and participation is among senior managers only. It is also true that managers do not encourage and invite participation, as they consider it a tool for demonstrating their own inadequacy. Participation in the private sector is further restricted. Profit-making corporations have tried to create some semblance of participation relatively more frequently than the loss-making corporations. Horizontal participation is common to most corporations, but vertical participation is rare.

Senior managers are kept too busy and involved in details, leaving little time and scope for thinking about their responsibilities. The government expects accountability but has not shown sufficient willingness to give to them commensurate authority. As a result no substantial decisions are made by the managers without consulting the appropriate ministry, or they are made after so much delay that the damage to the corporation has already been done. The prior approval of the ministry is essential on trivial issues, where even the petty officials tend to act funny and put the blame of delayed implementation on corporate management. While the managers have been made accountable to the ministry, the latter is not. Since the managers deal with the politicians they lead the corporations into disorderly states.

The corporate links with the government indicate control and the possibility of misuse. The ministries treat the corporations under them as their appendices. They instruct the corporation to do what they want in very set ways. They may also question the same action later at a convenient time. People also find it convenient to hide behind the system and blame others for any failures. In the case of the private sector, approximately 68 per cent of the top-level managers took the majority of decisions, as compared with the 25 per cent in the public sector. In the profit-making corporations, nearly 30 per cent top-level managers found it possible to make decisions as compared with the 20 per cent in the loss-making corporations. The process of decision-making is thus at a low key in the public sector.

Lack of Enough Work and Overmanning

Overmanning characterizes most public sector corporations, irrespective of the fact that a corporation may or may not generate profits. This phenomenon is a drain on the allocated resources, particularly in corporations which are in the red and incurring losses year after year. The situation in the private sector is not that gloomy. While one finds ample instances of people pretending to have a heavy workload and the employees up to a certain level making overtime, instances abound from all types of corporations demonstrating that very little is demanded of the employee or that the employees are assigned only nominal work. This leaves people with adequate time to indulge in all kinds of unproductive work activities. Those who find greener pastures leave, but those who remain continue to do the same thing year after year. The work processes are reported to be more efficient in the private (75 per cent), than in the public (40 per cent) sector. A higher percentage of the public sector managers (32 per cent) perceive the work processes as retrograde and degenerative, and little more so in the loss-making corporations.

In both the public and private sectors, the future perception of the output is not very optimistic. It is expected to involve either average or high cost.

Social-Welfare and Personnel Policies

A large number of managers in the public sector (65 per cent) have reported that if the corporations are seen as centres of production and profits they should not be burdened with the welfare objectives of the political system as is the current practice. The achievement of national and social objectives like the development of far-fetched geographical areas where the corporation is set up, taking over of sick enterprises, employment of SC/ST, landowners and the handicapped and the principle of employment generation cut deep into the profitability of corporations.

A large percentage of the managers in the public sector (52 per cent) report that despite deficits year after year the personnel policies are oriented towards self-development, and more so in the profit-making corporations. The percentage of managers in this group has been lower in the private sector (30 per cent). A higher percentage feel that the policy in the private sector is kept deliberately flexible (35 per cent) as the private sector thrives on this.

In the domain of human resource development and management, recruitment, placement and training are important. Most corporations recruit and place the managers, but leave the training to chance or do so only half-heartedly. The training function is important for the growth and sustenance of the corporation at all levels, beginning from the workers to the seniormost managers. It has been advocated that various in-house training and management development programmes should be made a formal feature of the organizational design itself. This is necessary to acquire new understanding, information and skills, and overall to enhance self-awareness. Training may also be used to generate commitment and conviction among employees. Once selected, even the topmen must be exposed to training. Attitudinal training is needed by all to keep pace with development.

10

OVERVIEW AND AHEAD

The public sector in India characterizes the planned socialist model of the national economy. It is the backbone of economic development and social progress. Politicians, planners and bureaucrats have invested not only large sums of money in this sector but also the hopes and aspirations of the people, which unfortunately continue to remain unrealized year after year. Low productivity, low capacity utilization, lower returns and industrial unrest continue to be the endemic features of the corporate sector, while the politicians, bureaucrats and managers all go in circles to find scapegoats in each other. There is concern but little positive action. There is the need to understand and analyze the problems of operation by using appropriate theoretical concepts and the need to identify appropriate strategies of development and turnaround. There is, however, lack of conviction and dearth of sound analytical frameworks. It is necessary to gainfully use the available theoretical concepts, and to test the relevance of these in practice by focusing on the perceptual experiences and self-reports of senior managers in the public and private sectors, and to identify an action plan. The objective here has been to examine if the sectoral identities, the profit status of the corporations and the personal orientations of senior managers relate to their time management, the time allocated to different work activities, the frequency of work taken home, the choice of strategies, the ability to deal with the environment, the choice of adopted structures, goal achievement, role perceptions, feelings of confidence and professional commitment. Further, can the variance in managers' time management, personal orientation, strategy-making, perceptions of environment and the structures account for major differences in goal achievement, role perceptions, confidence and professional commitment, and thus effectiveness in different types of corporations?

The evidence obtained in the project has only partly been in the expected direction, yet it is encouraging enough to grapple constructively with the riddles of socio-organizational realities. Time management in general fails to be a sufficiently differentiating source of variance either at the individual or at the corporate level, indicating that all managers conceptualize and use time in a fairly compatible manner. They spend comparable amounts of time on families, hobbies, personal care and social life. They function within the prescribed statutory provisions as far as the time spent on work is concerned. The emphasis is on beating the system, because of which they comply with the letter rather than the spirit of the system. The private sector managers put more emphasis on core work activities, while in the public sector peripheral activities are given priority. Time management at work in the public sector is tied to several structural factors, such as the overmanning of corporations, absence of direct accountability and higher job security. There are only nominal differences among managers in the choice of strategy-making, dealing with the environment and in the choice of structures. All managers have inclination towards externality. The line between internal and external orientation is very thin and blurred.

Time management is found less than optimal in all groups, and there is high externality in managers in both the sectors, demonstrating that all managers tend to feel that the causes of their success or failure lie in the external environment. They lack the necessary inner strength and confidence to manage their situational contingencies. They feel that the time delays and cost overruns on most projects are due to factors beyond their control. When they find they are unable to achieve their targets they feel nervous and often make midstream changes, which lead to more difficulties rather than solutions to the problems. It reflects their poor planning, inexperienced budgeting and lack of concern for the losses. The tendency to do so is much higher in the public sector and in loss-making corporations. This practice needs to be checked and reverted if possible. The policy should thus be to discourage and refrain from changes in projects which have been initiated. A thorough assessment of a plan/project should be done at the initial stage itself, and appropriate changes made if necessary.

Some sectoral differences are observed in the time management patterns. In the private sector some time is spent by managers on social life, on discussions with superiors and on having rounds of the workplaces, as compared with the significant amount of time given to paperwork, meetings and dealing with ministries in the public sector. It seems that much valuable time of top-level managers in the public sector is lost in paperwork and other superficial activities like endless discussions and unproductive meetings which gives them a sense of lower learning or no learning at the personal level. Needless to say, there is no advantage of such exercises at the corporate level. This does not justify the huge investments made in the public sector and the high hopes set on these corporations as temples of production. Rules and procedures often become ends in themselves and displace the system's goals. In terms of the institutionalization theory, many of the structural forms and processes are imported by these corporations only to make the system good enough for self-maintenance (DiMaggio and Powell, 1983) and to justify the way things are done (Ashworth and Gibbs, 1990).

In the private and public sectors, the role of strategies is seen relatively more relevant to goal achievement, clarity in role perceptions, confidence and professional commitment of managers than the environmental and structural constraints. The strategies are, however, used in different ways in the two sectors. The managers in the private sector use proactivity and risk-taking strategies to achieve higher goals, while the public sector managers use these strategies to maintain the status quo and to avert losses.

The strategies of futurity and innovation are used positively by managers in the two sectors which have higher clarity in role perceptions. The strategies of futurity and innovation are used in the public sector by managers having a high degree of confidence in handling the situation. All the four strategies are used in one way or the other by managers in two sectors. While each strategy is seen to have meaning in relation to a particular situation, there is no dominant trend in the choice of strategies in the public sector linked to effectiveness. Thus, it seems that managers in both the sectors, and more so in the public sector, ought to learn ways of using all the strategies to promote productive activities.

It emerges that the strategies, as Mintzberg (1987) has observed, can be vital to organizations, both by their presence and by their absence. The same strategies can be used by managers differently. These often reflect differences in the patterns of organizational socialization and in the acquired tactics of managers which they have found rewarding and best in their experiences. Dynamism is more in the public sector and heterogeneity in the environment is relevant in the private sector. Scanning is useful as a structural variable in the private sector.

Some areas of time management and the time allocated to work are found meaningfully related to aspects of strategy-making, environment and structure, goal achievement, role perceptions, confidence and professional commitment. Some aspects of strategy-making, environment and structure correlate differentially with each other and with goal achievement, role perceptions, confidence and professional commitment in different groups. A judicious management of one's time in some areas of life and work activities has a bearing on strategy-making, perceptions of environment and aspects of structure. Also, the types of strategies chosen by managers and the kinds of structures considered appropriate to deal with challenges in the environment have relevance for their overall effectiveness. Goal achievement, role perceptions, confidence and professional commitment are found positively related with each other, indicating that all are equally good indices of managerial effectiveness. These can be used together with the objective indicators of organizational effectiveness in evolving appropriate policies to strengthen the managers' self-perceptions.

The personal orientation of managers is little more important in profit-making corporations for goal achievement, confidence and professional commitment, than in the loss-making corporations. The use of the proactive and futurity strategies is found related to goal achievement and to feeling confident. The perceptions of heterogeneity in environment and differentiated structures are associated with professional commitment of managers. In the loss-making corporations the time allocated to social life is related to goal achievement of managers; differentiated structures are related to goal achievement and the clarity of role perceptions; taking work home frequently is related to feeling confident and professionally committed; the futurity strategy is negatively related to goal achievement, and the innovation strategy is related to confidence.

The use of the futurity strategy by the internality-oriented managers is associated with clear role perceptions, higher confidence and professional commitment. The proactivity strategy is related to goal achievement. The time they put in having rounds of factories and offices and in planning and managing contributes to their goal achievement. The time spent by the externality-oriented managers in meeting their social obligations and the frequency of work taken home are helpful in goal achievement, feeling confident and being professionally committed. The use of the innovation strategy helps in role clarity and confidence.

The variance in role perceptions, confidence and professional commitment is found better explained by the selected aspects of time management, time allocated to various work activities, strategy-making, environment, structure and personal orientation of managers than goal achievement, in both the private and public sectors. To some extent, this seems to be related to the nature of these indicators, which are formed on the basis of self-assessments of managers. It is possible that these are manipulated by managers to a good extent to meet the contingencies, while the achievement of goals is highly dependent on numerous other considerations. The support is not necessarily contingent on either their capability or on outcomes. Many other policy considerations are likely to be involved. Moreover, it seems from the logic of operation of corporations in the two sectors that the control environment of organizations is quite a potent regulating variable of managerial effectiveness. These policies could include the implementation of the Monopolies and Restrictive Trade Practices Act (MRTP), and the control of business houses and requirements imposed by financial institutions in the case of the private sector (Khurana, 1981; Bidani and Mitra, 1982; Pendse, 1983); the state regulatory apparatus and the national policies in the case of the public sector (Chaudhuri et al., 1982; Khandwalla, 1982; Paul, 1983).

Some differences in the explanatory power of time management, aspects of strategy, environment and structure are observed by the sector type, the profit status of corporations and the personal orientation of managers. The sectoral differences confirm the profit versus maintenance or the synergetic versus soft orientation of the two types of management, leading to differences in allocations and choices. While it would be desirable for both to have profit and development as the primary goals, it is not so in practice. The emphasis on keeping the different sections happy, excessive controls and political interference have directly caused increased corruption, loss of production and inefficiency in the public sector, and have cost the private sector indirectly by creating pressure to invest regularly in routine and unproductive operations. A balance between liberalization and controls ought to be sought by keeping in view that retrograde practices used in one sector will necessarily enter into the functioning of the other sector, and will ultimately lower the levels of achievement.

The corporate culture in the public sector is soft and maintenance-oriented, when compared with the somewhat performance-oriented culture of the private sector. The peripheral activities like paperwork and meetings consume so much of the time of the seniormost and top-level managers in the public sector corporations, that the core activities like planning are not given adequate attention. These tend to be seen as the myths of rational decision-making. Decisions are rarely made at the right time. The industrial policy must focus on a likely transformation of the work culture, and must ask for the provision of inputs needed in that direction, such as the time managers should give to planning for problem solving and question seeking.

The public sector has also suffered from the problem of succession, because of which many corporations tend to remain without topmen for long periods. The public sector does not have a policy of succession for the topmen who set the tone for the corporation. This implies the indifference and half-heartedness of politicians and administrators towards the public sector. On the contrary, the issue of succession is taken much more seriously in the private sector and worked out in advance. It acts as a demoralizing/weakening influence on those who are likely to succeed the top-level managers, and makes them inactive and indecisive. Given the condition of 'social loafing around' and wasting time, the employees and unions take full advantage of the situation and negate the work ethics of the people who work. The public sector is in need of a clear-cut policy about the appointment of a new chairman while the outgoing one is still in office.

The private sector, to a limited extent and the public sector, invariably, are tied to difficult policies and legislations. The achievement of equity and social justice by providing development in far-fetched areas, the provision of jobs for the 'sons of the soil' and the recruitment of minimally qualified people from the reserved categories are undoubtedly noble goals, but the implementation of these to derive political mileage have landed the corporations in an unbelievable mess. The objectives of equity and social justice are overexploited by politicians and bureaucrats. This leads to overmanning, group conflicts, unionization, unproductive work climate, and the devaluation of merit and efficiency. These problems have to be realistically diagnosed, understood and solved in a cooperative manner by using the positive strategies of growth and development of both individuals and corporations. The policies and practices of recruitment, promotion and performance appraisal ought to be periodically re-examined, and the contentious issues resolved through wider debates and discussions.

The managers in the public sector are as professionally qualified and competent, confident of achieving their goals and clear about their roles as their counterparts in the private sector. They have comparable social origins and are trained in similar institutions. The differences in their functioning thus relate to their organizational socialization after recruitment to the manner of using opportunities and their competence, the extent of decentralization of authority, the variety of risks associated with functioning in a protracted environment, the overall corporate cultures, and the lack of accountability and performance. Managers often find it difficult to make rationally informed decisions. Information is seldom factual in the sense of being objective. All information systems are inevitably selective and require decision-making. When it is appropriate, managers often choose to ignore the detailed information and rely on intuition and gut feelings. Managers in the public and private sectors have clear perceptions of their roles, are confident, and professionally committed, and use similar strategies and structural mechanisms, but the two use them differently—in one to maintain the status quo and in the other to show results. As a result, when considering the huge investments in the public sector, one finds that the proportionate returns are much lower than in the private sector. In fact, the policy of indifference and deliberate avoidance adopted by the political bosses and bureaucrats to address these issues have landed the public sector into a precarious financial situation. Even in the best functioning industries the profits are an outcome of the protected and controlled market. The corporations have not developed structural and functional capabilities to be operative in a dynamic, open and competitive market economy. The organizational socialization tactics in the public sector need to be thoroughly reviewed and updated, and the policy ought to be made more supportive and growth-oriented.

The powerful effect of the socio-cultural milieu is visible in the comparable use of time and strategies acquired by all managers as universal values. In Indian society, there is an overemphasis on the past and a lack of orientation towards the future. Although the high level of education and the professional preparation of managers have changed their orientations to a certain extent, they have not internalized these values, and these are not manifested in their work behaviour. In the face of difficult situations and the failure to control losses they find it easy to take refuge in the achievements of the past. They tend to look at time, like everyone else, as something ever present and static. Delays in action and loss of time in reaching targets and meeting deadlines are easily tolerated, making them learn the bureaucratic method of stalling, without even having a sense of guilt. The unstated purpose of political control has overshadowed the primary economic objective of the corporations. The policy implication seems to be the need of a clear focus on the stated purposes and goals of public sector corporations and the translation of these into clear operational terms.

The human resource development (HRD) function in most corporations is weak and inadequate. People have inadequate communication. They have misunderstandings and mistrust. The HRD function ought to be developed in the proper perspective. The policies of recruitment, selection and training, and career development need to be related to the needs of the industry.

Theoretically, most managers showed an awareness of the need to improve the working of corporations, but their efforts in practice varied. A group leader of a profit-making corporation was able to demonstrate, with the help of charts, how he had taken up the Integrated Management Control System (IMCS) to control delays and cut costs. Some of the factors outlined in his plan included: implicit faith in planning and monitoring, appropriate work culture and environment, timely development of infrastructures, delegation of powers, clear demarcation of responsibility, identification of central and state agencies for coordination, development of team spirit, motivation, accessible top management, reward system, participative approach with contractors, early identification of all unconventional facilities, advance action for procurement of building materials, safety, housekeeping, clear-cut decisions etc.

Similarly, the managing director of a loss-making corporation trying to achieve a turnaround identified the steps outlined for changing the work culture of the organization. These were: restructuring of the organizational set-up, participative management and motivation of employees, human resource development, manpower planning and control, productivity improvement, control of inventories, quality improvement, pollution control, computerization of management information systems, marketing and sales etc. Some corporations in the private sector have introduced regular employee attitude surveys and the concept of profit centres.

The recent measures of the Government of India as envisaged in the New Industrial Policy (NIP, 1991) aim to do away with the system of excessive licensing and to follow a policy of liberalization. This indicates the intentions of the powers that be to seek a balance between ideology and economic forces in the national and international markets. The New Industrial Policy aims at:

1. Self-reliance to build on the many-sided gains already made.
2. Encouragement to Indian entrepreneurship, promotion of productivity and employment generation.
3. Development of indigenous technology through greater investment in R & D and bringing in new technology to help Indian manufacturing units attain world standards.
4. Removing regulatory systems and other weaknesses.
5. Increasing the competitiveness of industries for the benefit of the common man.
6. Incentives for industrialization of backward areas.
7. Enhanced support to the small-scale industries sector.
8. Ensure running of public sector undertakings (PSUs) on business lines and cut their losses.
9. Protect the interests of workers.
10. Abolish the monopoly of any sector in any field of manufacture, except on strategic or security grounds.
11. To link Indian economy to the global market so that the country can acquire the ability to pay for its imports, and be less dependent on foreign aid.

The 'whiff' of liberalization outlined in the New Industrial Policy promises to abolish many of the unnecessary controls that should demolish partially the bureaucratic machinery that has determined the economic fate of the country for so long. The managers in both sectors have new and different economic and strategic challenges ahead, and would have to grow out of strong shields and face the perils of competition at home and abroad, and either profit or pay the price for their own inefficiency and mistakes. Freedom is always two-pronged, and it should be understood as such. It involves responsibilities and also penalties, and the managers have the task of seeking a balance. It is their responsibility and vision to energize themselves and their corporations and to go beyond the maintenance of status quo to achieve some predetermined standards.

This is close to what Mintzberg (1991) has expressed in favour of the balancing of various competitive and conflicting forces to make organizations effective. To him a manager has to be a Peterian and a Porterian, and perhaps more at the same time, as the achievement of a balance and long-term sustenance of these forces are the crux of managerial effectiveness.

The available theoretical perspectives of role, goal and development approach have been found only of limited use in explaining the threats and challenges to managerial effectiveness in both sectors, as the socio-organizational realities of managers and corporations are much more complex. Some of the components of the hierarchic and profession theories are also found useful. Managers do perform administrative functions, accept status, are professionally committed at the personal level, and are authority figures, but they do not acquire and transmit knowledge to others to a satisfactory extent, and rarely do they take independent actions.

Irrespective of the sector, profit status and the personal orientation of managers, the conceptual model of managerial effectiveness used for analysis has been found quite adequate and flexible in explaining the role of personal, social and organizational factors. It is true that managers should like to achieve more in less time, and attain economies of effort and resource expenditure. One possible suggestion is for managers to manage their time well by adopting appropriate strategies in managing the contextual problems. They should not deal with problems in isolation or in parts, but in their entirety. They should ask themselves what additional issues should be explicated in order to give them greater awareness and alternative strategies, while dealing with the corporate problems at hand in an integrated manner. They should spend adequate time in understanding the crucial problems and the domain of influence of these to monitor/avoid occasional fallouts.

They should understand the criticality of their roles and the team's role in achieving the strategic success of the corporation they are in. The responsibility is collective and the initiative should be taken by them as group leaders. They should be creative and far-reaching in identifying the options and strategies, and not ambivalent in decision-making. They have to be tough-minded to be able to bring the teams into alignment with the needs and the context of operation of corporations, and yet sensitive to the personal and social needs of employees at different levels. They have to understand the constraints on resources and job performance, and have the necessary flexibility and fluidity to be able to creatively rethink, and monitor the initiated plan of action that can avoid time and cost overruns. Midway changes in the ongoing projects are found in general to be more costly than introducing another complementary project and thus should not be made. All senior managers should feel and act with conviction that the corporation is theirs and any wastage will be of their resources only. They should find effective ways of communicating this message to corporate managers, political bosses, bureaucrats and other stakeholders.

Planners, politicians and managers should accept and appreciate the embeddedness of people, events and organizations within the social system, where a change at one point causes ripples at numerous points in myriad and unanticipated ways. Effective organizations conform to a limited number of more or less coherent gestalts of power, strategy, structure, subsystems and core values (Greenwood and Hinings, 1988). Managers at all levels need to pursue humanistic values in the design and operation of systems, such as acceptance of inquiry, expanded consciousness and recognition of choice, collaboration, mutual help and authenticity.

In the prevalent political and economic scenario it does not seem likely that a large-scale privatization of existing public sector corporations can take place. It has many barriers and perils as there is no clear exit policy. There are problems of adequate resources, opposition from organized labour and political compulsions. The functioning of the public sector units needs to be streamlined. The mechanism of Memorandum of Understanding may be used as a tool of control. The public sector's existence is vital for tackling the national problems of poverty, malnutrition, unemployment, shelter, rural-urban divide, regional disparities and illiteracy. The mixed economy model has to be pursued and the two sectors have to coexist and cooperate in a more competitive manner.

It is hoped that in the changed business context the proposed analytical model will yield better prediction. With this optimism, it may be left to future researchers and managers to make the most effective use of these findings for promoting planned behaviour among managers and for creating appropriate social, political and legal conditions of functioning in corporations and for socializing the managers and employees to suit the desired goals and corporate cultures.

Appendix I
The Questionnaire

PART I

1. We are all aware that effective management is management of one's time in an optimal manner. Given the fact that one has only 24 hours in a day at one's disposal, how do you distribute your time on an average working day. Respond either in hours or in percentage of time.

    (a) Family-related activities_____
    (b) Hobbies_____
    (c) Social life_____
    (d) Work and related activities_____
    (e) Sleeping and personal care, etc._____
    (f) Any other_____

2. How much time do you spend in your workplace on:

    (a) Discussions with superiors_____
    (b) Discussions with juniors and peers_____
    (c) Planning and managing_____
    (d) Paperwork_____
    (e) Sit-in meetings_____
    (f) Having a round of office/factory_____
    (g) Sorting out with ministry officials etc._____
    (h) Knowing about market trends_____
    (i) Any other activities_____

3. How often do you have to spend extra time on the job:

    (a) Almost every day_____
    (b) Two or three times a week_____
    (c) Never_____

4. Keeping an ideal situation of 100 per cent achievement in view, where do you place your achievement of:

(a) Targeted corporate goals—20% & below, 30%, 40%, 50%, 60%, 70%, 80%+.
(b) Achieved corporate goals—20% & below, 30%, 40%, 50%, 60%, 70%, 80%+.
(Indicate by using a tick mark √)

5. In this Company, and specifically in your position, how clear are you about the following:	Below 20%	20–40%	40–60%	60–80%	80% and above
(a) Your job responsibilities.					
(b) Your authority to do different things.					
(c) The expectations of your seniors.					
(d) The expectations of your juniors.					
(e) The amount of freedom you have to make decisions.					
(f) The skills your job requires.					
(g) The benefits and entitlements you may have.					
(h) Your power potential to reward juniors.					
(i) The extent to which you can insist on your point of view.					
(j) Your ability to take seniors, colleagues and juniors with you.					
(k) Your ability to recognize the work of your juniors.					

6. I feel confident of myself:

	Below 20%	20–40%	40–60%	60–80%	80% and above
(a) Generally speaking, as a senior manager.					
(b) When I deal with my boss to resolve the problems related to work.					
(c) Even when some managers feel in full control of their situation and others don't feel so confident.					
(d) In overcoming troubles in my unit.					
(e) While discussing with the 'Board of Directors' the problems I face at work.					
(f) In trying to make new friends.					
(g) In trying to meet the performance standards set for me.					
(h) When I am given recognition for the work I do.					
(i) In seeking support of the top administration in solving problems at work.					
(j) When I am faced with disagreements with the top executive on a crucial issue.					
(k) When I am faced with disagreements with the labour union on a crucial issue.					

	Below 20%	20–40%	40–60%	60–80%	80% and above
(l) In making my job a success.					
(m) In dealing with my fellow executives and resolving our problems on a mutual basis.					

7. I like:

	Below 20%	20–40%	40–60%	60–80%	80% and above
(a) To make use of my knowledge and skills.					
(b) To learn about new strategies and solutions.					
(c) To work with my colleagues of superior professional competence.					
(d) To earn professional reputation.					
(e) To work on complex and challenging tasks.					
(f) To try new ideas.					

8. Express the extent of your agreement to the following statements by keeping your company in view.

	Below 20%	20–40%	40–60%	60–80%	80% and above
(a) Our production methods have changed very substantially over the last 5 years.					
(b) There is a strong emphasis on the marketing of true and tried products.					
(c) No new lines of products have been added in the past 5 years.					

	Below 20%	20–40%	40–60%	60–80%	80% and above
9(a) We strongly prefer low-risk projects.					
(b) Due to the nature of the industrial environment it is best to explore it gradually and cautiously.					
10(a) There is a strong tendency to follow the market leader in introducing new products.					
(b) We are oriented towards growth, innovation and development.					
11(a) Decisions aimed at exploiting opportunities are most common.					
(b) There is a bird-in-the-hand emphasis in management decisions.					
(c) We plan long-term investments.					
(d) We plan for human resource development.					
(e) We adopt new techniques of organizational efficiency					

	Below 20%	20–40%	40–60%	60–80%	80% and above
12(a) Our company must change its marketing practices to keep pace with the market needs.					
(b) The rate at which products are getting obsolete in this industry is very fast.					
(c) The actions of policymakers are easy to predict.					
(d) Demand and supply of products is fairly easy to match.					
(e) The methods and techniques of production in industry change in a major way.					
13(a) Our company is not diversified and caters to fixed buyers.					
(b) Our production does not match the purchasing capacity of customers.					
(c) All our products face the same kind of competition (difficult/ easy).					
(d) Our different products utilize different methods of production.					

	Below 20%	20–40%	40–60%	60–80%	80% and above
14(a) We gather opinions from clients on a routine basis.					
(b) We track explicit policies and tactics of competitors.					
(c) We use special market research studies.					
(d) In decision-making, there is great reliance on personnel with experience and commonsense.					
(e) The company employs very few professionals such as engineers and accountants.					

15. To what extent does your company forecast the following:

(a) Resources (availability)					
(b) Nature of market					
(c) Technology					
(d) Sales					
(e) Profits					
(f) Customer preferences					

	Less than 3	3–5	5–7	7–9	9 & above
16(a) How many unrelated product lines does your company market?					

	Below 20%	20–40%	40–60%	60–80%	80% and above
(b) To what extent do your products use very similar processes/techniques?					
(c) Do your products use very similar marketing strategies, types of customers, pricing etc.					

APPENDIX II
SOME CRITICAL INCIDENTS

A few outstanding critical incidents which reflected on the professionalism and work behaviour of senior managers are included below. The sole intention is that those who read this may refrain from indulging in such practices. Full care is taken to ensure objectivity in reporting these cases and the confidentiality of the corporate bodies employing them.

1. The executive made an appointment, but was not available in his office, he left no information with his personal assistant (PA) for us. Three weeks later we happened to be in the area and decided to drop in and see if he was in the office. A person typing in the cabin outside his office said that he was in the office and that we could meet him. Then his PA appeared and told us to wait outside as he would have to inform and seek the permission of his boss. He went in and came out within a few seconds to say that we could not meet him as the boss was very busy and would be going out soon. On our repeated requests, we were allowed to talk to him on the phone, and he readily agreed to meet us for precisely 15 minutes. The executive apologized to us for his mistake in not informing us beforehand and spent nearly an hour and 45 minutes in answering our questions. He apparently did not have any meeting to attend.

2. We had interviewed an executive about two weeks earlier. He had taken the questionnaire so that he could complete it in his leisure time and return it to us later. We went to him to find out about the questionnaire. We came to know from the office that he had passed it on to a junior officer to do it on his behalf. We decided to meet the executive and tell him that it was not part of the delegation of work. He then agreed to do the questionaire himself in our presence. He told us about two others in the corporation who had done the same thing. We discarded their questionnaires and made them complete fresh ones, this time in our presence.

3. The discussion with the director had just begun. Suddenly, an excited

executive (A) came into the room with some papers in his hand and said: 'I have to inform you that even though you asked me to prepare this paper in the morning I was told that executive (B) has also been asked to do it. Why?' The director said apologetically that he had not done so and requested executive (A) to prepare the necessary document.

4. The researcher entered the room of the director and was immediately asked: 'What brings you here?' After explaining to him the purpose of the visit and the research objectives, he took the questionnaire and began to read it. He just looked at it and said: 'I am really amused to see this. How useless an exercise this is. Am I going to rate myself below 100 per cent on anything and expose my weaknesses? Let me ask you: "How do you rate yourself?"' He began reading the questions and shouted for a quick response. The executive not only lacked courtesy, but demonstrated to the hilt his frustrations, his hatred for self and others and his thorough cynicism. He observed that in the midst of sharks, he was trying to achieve good results. He said he should never be interviewed again as he was a perfect man and was looking for perfection in a world of corrupt people.

REFERENCES

Abdel-Halim, A.A. (1980). Effects of Person Job Compatibility on Managerial Reactions to Role Ambiguity. *Organizational Behavior and Human Performance*, 26: 193-211.

Abramson, I.Y., Seligman, M.E.P. and Teasdale, J.D. (1978). Learned Helplessness in Humans: Critique and Reformulation. *Journal of Abnormal Psychology*, 87: 49-74.

Agarwal, N.M. (1984). Determinants of Intergenerational Conflict in Organizations. *Vikalpa*, 9: 121-34.

Agarwal, R. (1974). Organization Structure and Communication in a Manufacturing sector in India. *Indian Journal of Industrial Relations*, 9: 385-86.

Aguilar, F.J. (1967). *Scanning the Business Environment*. New York: MacMillan.

Anderson, C.R. (1977). Locus of Control, Coping Behaviors and Performances in a Stress Setting: A Longitudinal Study. *Journal of Applied Psychology*, 62: 446-51.

Anderson, C. and Paine, F. (1975). Managerial Perceptions and Strategic Behavior. *Academy of Management Journal*, 18: 811-23.

Anderson, C.R., Hellriegel, D. and Slocum, J.W. Jr. (1977). Managerial Response to Environmentally Induced Stress. *Academy of Management Journal*, 10: 160-272.

Ashworth, B.E. and Gibbs, B.W. (1990). The Double-edge of Organizational Legitimation. *Organization Science*, 1: 177-94.

Balakrishnan, K., Bhargava, S. and Jain, V.P. (1980). *A Comparative Study of the Growth and Strategy of Two Large Indian Business Houses (Birlas and Tatas)*. Ahmedabad: Indian Institute of Management.

Balakrishnan, S. and Wernerfelt, B.P (1986). Technical Change, Competition and Vertical Integration. *Strategic Management Journal*, 7: 347-59.

Bandura, A. (1977). *Social Learning Theory*. Englewood Cliffs, NJ: Prentice Hall.

———(1986). *Social Foundations of Thought and Action: A Social Cognitive Theory*. Englewood Cliffs, NJ: Prentice Hall.

———(1988). Self-regulation of Motivation and Action Through Goal Systems. In V. Hamilton, G.H. Bower and N.H. Frijda (Eds.) *Cognitive Perspectives on Emotion and Motivation*. Dondrecht, the Netherlands: Kluver Academic.

Bartunek, J., Gordon, J., and Weathersby, R. (1983). Developing Completed Understanding in Administration. *Academy of Management Review*, 8: (2), 2173-284.

Bass, B.M. (1985) *Leadership and Performance Beyond Expectations.* New York: The Free Press.

Bateman, T.S. and Zeithaml, C.P. (1989). The Psychological Context of Strategic Decisions: A Model and Convergent Experimental Findings. *Stratetic Management Journal,* 10: 59-74.

Becker, H.S. (1960). Notes on the Concept of Commitment. *American Journal of Sociology,* 66: 32-40.

Bedeian, A.G., Armenakis, A.A. and Curran, S.M. (1980). Personality Correlates of Role Stress. *Psychological Reports,* 46: 627-32.

Beehr, T. and Newman, J. (1978). Job Stress, Employee Health aand Organizational Effectiveness: A Facet Analysis, Model and Literature Review. *Personnel Psychology,* 31: 665-700.

Bennis, W.G. (1966). The Concept of Organizational Health. In W.G. Bennis (Ed.) *Changing Organizations.* New York: McGraw-Hill.

Bennis, W.G. and Nanus, B. (1985). *Leaders: The Strategies for Taking Charge,* New York: Harper & Row.

Bidani, S. and Mitra, P.K. (1982). *Industrial Sickness: Identification and Rehabilitation.* New Delhi: Vision Books.

Blake, R.R. and Mouton, J.S. (1964). *The Managerial Grid.* Houston, TX: Gulf Publishing.

Bluedorn, A.C. (1980). Cutting the Gordian Knot: A Critique of the Effectiveness Tradition in Organization Research. *Sociology and Social Research,* 64: 477-96.

Bourgeois, L.J. (1980). Performance and Consensus. *Strategic Management Journal.* 1:227-48.

Boyd, B. (1990). Corporate Linkages and Organizational Environment: A Test of the Resource Dependence Model. *Strategic Management Journal* 11: 419-30.

Bradford, D.L. and Cohen, A.R. (1984). *Managing for Excellence.* New York: John Wiley.

Brown, L.D. (1984). Effective Change Strategies for Public Enterprises: Lessons from Turnaround Cases. *Vikalpa,* 9: 97-112.

Burns, T. and Stalker, G.M. (1961). *The Management of Innovation. London:* Tavistock.

Cameron, K.S. (1978). Measuring Organizational Effectiveness in Institutions of Higher Education. *Administrative Science Quarterly,* 23: 604-32.

Cameron, K.S. (1979). Evaluating Organizational Effectiveness in Organized Anarchies. Paper presented at the Academy of Management, Atlanta, GA.

———(1984) Organizational Culture in a Post-Industrial Environment: An Expansion of Life Cycle Model of Organizational Development. Paper presented at the Academy of Management, Boston, MA.

———(1986a). Effectiveness as Paradox: Consensus and Confiict in Conceptions of Organizational Effectiveness. *Management Science.* 32 (5): 539-53.

———(1986b). A Study of Organizational Effectiveness and its Predictors. *Management Science* 32: 87-112.

Cameron, K.S. and Whetten, D.A (1983). Organizational Effectiveness: One Model or Several? In K.S. Cameron and D.A. Whetten (Eds.), *Organizational Effectiveness: A Comparison of Multiple Models.* New York: Academic Press. 1-24.

Campbell, J.P. (1977). On the Nature of Organizational Effectiveness. In P.S. Goodman and J.M. Pennings (Eds.) *New Perspectives on Organizational Effectiveness.* San Francisco: Jossey-Bass, 13-55.

Carter, N.(1991). Learning to Measure Performance: The Use of Indicators in Organization. *Public Administration,* 69: 85-101.

Chaganti, R.R. (1979). Innovations in Government Organizations: A Comparative Review. *ASCI Journal of Management,* 9: 19-32.

Chakraborty, S. and Dixit, S. (1992). Developing a Turnaround Strategy. A Case Study Approach. *Omega, International Journal of Management Science* 20 (3): 345-52.

Chandler, A.D. (1962). *Strategy and Structure.* Cambridge, MA: MIT Press.

Chaturvedi, A. (1980). Organizational Effectiveness and some Issues. *Indian Journal of Public Administration,* 26: 1017-40.

Chaudhury, S. (1980). Acquisition and Assimilation of Technology in the Tractor Industry in India: The Strategic Perspective. Unpublished doctoral dissertation, Indian Institute of Management, Ahmedabad.

Chaudhury, S., and Khandwalla, P.N. (1983). Management of Diversification in Public Enterprises. *Institute of Public Enterprise Journal,* 6: 41-66.

Choudhury, S., Kumar, K., Prahlad, C.K. and Vathsala, S. (1982). Patterns of Diversification in Larger Indian Enterprises. *Vikalpa,* 7: 23-39.

Chomsky, Noam. (1957). *Syntactic Structures.* The Hague: Mouton.

Cohen, M., Jaffray, J.Y. and Said, T. (1985). Individual Behavior Under Risk and Under Certainty: An Experimental Study. *Theory and Decision,* 18: 203-28.

Collins, T. and Moore, D. (1970). *The Organization Makers.* New York: Appleton-Century-Crofts.

Connolly, T., Conlon, E.J. and Deutch, S.J. (1980). Organizational Effectiveness: A Multiple Constituency Approach. *Academy of Management Review,* 5: 211-17.

Coyne, J.C., Metalsky, G.I. and Lavelle, T.L. (1980). Learned Helplessness as Experimenter-induced Failure and its Alleviation with Attention Redeployment. *Journal of Abnormal Psychology,* 89: 350-57.

Cummings, L.L. (1983). Organizational Effectiveness and Organizational Behavior: A Critical Perspective. In K.S. Cameron and D.A. Whetten (Eds.) *Organizational Effectiveness: A Comparison of Multiple Models.* New York: Academic Press.

Daft, R.L. and Lengel, R.H. (1984). Information Richness: A New Approach to Managerial Behavior and Organizational Design. *Research in Organization Behaviour,* 6: 191-233.

Dahlback, Olof (1990). Personality and Risk-taking. *Personality and Individual Differences.* 11: 1235-42.

Darasse, C. (1988). Time Perspective and Organizational Involvement. *Applied Psychology: An International Review,* 37(4): 411-25.

Das, T.K. (1986). *The Subjective Side of Strategy Making.* New York: Praeger.

Dayal, I. (1967). Constraint of Legislation on Organizational Effectiveness. *Indian Journal of Industrial Relations,* 2: 315-33.

———(1973). Planned Changes in Organization. *Administrative Change,* 1: 29-31.

———(1984). Effective Management: Looking Within. *Indian Management,* 52: 24-25.

de Lecea, F.J.R.M. (1982). Premilinary study of Values: The Case of Spain (Mimeo). Madrid, Spain.

Devellis, R.F., McEvoy Devellis, B. and McCauley, C. (1978). Vicarious Acquisition of Learned Helplessness. *Journal of Personality and Social Psychology,* 36: 894-99.

DiMaggio, P.J. and Powell, W.W. (1983). The Iron Cage Revisited: Institutional Isomorphism and Collective Rationality in Organizational Fields. *American Sociological Review* 48: 147-60.

Downey, K.D., Hellriegel, D. and Slocum, J. Jr. (1977). Individual Characteristics as Sources of Perceived Uncertainty Variability. *Human Relations,* 30: 161-74.

Drucker, P. (1976). The Bored Board., *The Wharton Magazine.* Wharton Business School, Pennsylvania State University, Pennsylvania.

D'Souza, K.C. (1984). Organizations as Agents of Social Change. *Vikalpa,* 9: 233-47.

Duncan, R. (1972). Characteristics of Organizational Environments and Perceived Environmental Uncertainity. *Administrative Science Quarterly,* 17: 313-27.

Dutt, R. C. (1981). Public Enterprises: Prospects and Constraints for the Eighties. In Raj K. Nigam. (Ed.) (1981). *Eighties for the Public Sector.* New Delhi: Documentation Centre for Corporate and Business Policy Research.

Etzioni, A. (1964). *Modern Organizations. Englewood Cliffs, NJ: Prentice Hall.*

Evans, P.A.L. (1986). The Strategic Outcomes of Human Resource management. *Human Resource Management,* 25(1): 149-62.

Evans, P. and Bartolome, F. (1986). The Dynamics of Work-family Relationships on Managerial Lives. *International Review of Applied Psychology,* 35: 371-95.

Fisher, D., Merron, K. and Torbert, W.R. (1987). Human Development and Managerial Effectiveness. *Group and Organizational Studies.* 12(3): 257-73.

FORE (Foundation for Organization Research) (1984) *A Study of the Indicators and Process of Effectiveness Management.* New Delhi: FORE.

Fredrickson, J.W. (1983). Strategic Process Research: Questions and Recommendations. *Academy of Management Review,* 8: 565–75.

————(1984). The Comprehensiveness of Stratetic Decision Processes: Extension, Observations, Future Directions. *Academy of Management Journal* 27: 445-66.

————(1985). Effects of Decision Motive and Organizational Performance Level on Stratetic Decision Processes. *Academy of Management Journal,* 28: 821-43.

————(1986). The Strategic Decision Process and Organizational Structure. *Academy of Management Review,* 11: 280-97.

Galbraith, J.R. (1973). *Designing Complex Organizations.* Reading, MA: Addison–Wesley.

————(1977). *Organizational Design.* New York: Addison–Wesley.

Gall, M.D. (1988). *Making the Grade,* Rocklin, CA: Prima.

George, P.P. (1984). Diversified Indian Companies: A Study of Strategies and Financial Peformance. Unpublished doctoral dissertation. Ahmedabad: Indian Institute of Management.

Getzels, J.W. and Guba, E.G. (1955). Role Conflict and Personality. *Journal of Personality,* 24: 74-85.

Goodstadt, B.E. and Hjelle, L.A. (1973). Power to the Powerless: Locus of control and the use of power. *Journal of Personality and Social Psychology,* 27: 190-96.

Goodstein, L. (1983). Managers, Values and Organizational Development.*Group and Organizational Studies,* 8(2): 203-20.

Gouldner, A.W. (1957). Cosmos and Locals: Toward an Analysis of Latent Social Roles. *Administrative Science Quarterly,* 2: 444-80.

Government of India (1948). *Industrial Policy Resolution.* 6 April, 1(3)-44(13)/48, New Delhi.

————(1956). *Industrial Policy Resolution.* 30 April, 91/CF/48, New Delhi.

————(1980). 'Industrial Policy Resolution' 24 July, *Economic Survey 1980-81* New Delhi.

————(1991) 'New Industrial Policy' *Reserve Bank of India—Annual Report 1990-91* Ministry of Finance, Economic Division, New Delhi

Greenwood, R. and Hinings, C.R. (1988). Organizational Design Types, Tracks and the Dynamics of Strategy Change. *Organization Studies* 9: 293-36.

Hage, J. and Aiken, M. (1967). Program Change and Organizational Properties: A Comparative Analysis. *American Journal of Sociology.* 72: 503-19.

Hales, C.P. (1986). What do Managers do? A Critical Review of the Evidence. *Journal of Management Studies.* 21(1): 88-118.

Hall, R.H. (1967). Organizational Considerations in the Professional-organizational Relationship. *Administrative Science Quarterly,* 12: 461-78.

Hambrick, D.C. (1979). Environmental Scanning, Organizational Strategy and Executive Roles: a study in Three Industries. Unpublished Ph.D. Dissertation, Pennsylvania State University.

————(1981) Environment Strategy and Power within Top Management Teams. *Administrative Science Quarterly,* 26: 253-75.

Hamner, C. and Tosi, H. (1974), Relationships of Role Conflict and Role Ambiguity to Job Involvement Measurers. *Journal of Applied Psychology.* 59: 497-99.

Harkins, S.G. and Jackson, J.M. (1985). The Role of Evaluation in Eliminating Social Loafing. *Personality and Social Psychology Bulletin,* 11: 457-65.

Harkins, S. and Petty, R. (1982). Effects of Task Difficulty and Task Uniqueness on Social Loafing. *Journal of Personality and Social Psychology,* 43: 1214-29.

Harrison, F. (1974). The Management of Scientists: Determinants of Perceived Role Performance. *Academy of Management Journal,* 17: 234-41.

Hersey, P. and Blanchard K. (1982). *Management of Organizatiional Behavior* (4th Ed.). Englewood Cliff, NJ: Prentice Hall.

Hickson, D.J., Pugh, D.S. and Pheysey, D. (1969). Operations Technology and Organization Structure: An Empirical Reappraisal. *Administrative Science Quarterly.* 14: 378-97.

Holland, P. (1986). Competency Based Management and Style: How do You Manage? *Arab Banker,* 6(5): 22-23.

Homans, G. (1958). Social Behavior as Exchange. *American Journal of Sociology,* 63: 597-606.

Horton, T.R. (1986). *What Works for Me.* New York: Random House.

Huber, G.P. and McDaniel, R.R. (1986a). The Decision-making Paradigm of Organizational Design. *Management Science,* 32: 572-89.

————(1986b). Exploiting Information Technologies to Design More Effective Organizations. In M. Jarke (Ed.) *Managers, Micros and Main Frames.* New York: John Wiley.

Jauch, L., Gluck, W.F. and Obsorn, R.N.(1978). Organizational Loyality, Professional Commitment and Academic Research Productivity. *Academy of Management Journal,* 84-92.

Kahn, W.A. (1990a). Psychological Conditions of Personal Engagement and Disengagement at Work. *Academy of Management Journal,* 33(4): 692-724.

————(1990b). An Exercise of Authority. *Organizational Behavior Teaching Review,* 14(2): 28-42.

Kahn, R.L., Wolfe, D.M., Quinn, R.P., Snoek, J.D. and Rosenthal R.A. (1964). *Organizational Stress: Studies in Role Conflict and Ambiguity.* New York: John Wiley.

Kakar, S. (1972). Rationality and Irrationality of Business Leadership. *Journal of Business Policy,* 2:2.

Kanter, R.M. (1968). Commitment and Social Organization: A Study of Commitment Mechanisms in Utopian Communities. *American Sociological Review,* 33: 499-517.

Kanungo, R.N. (1990). Culture and Work Alienation. Western Models and Eastern Realities. *International Journal of Psychology,* 25: 795-812.

Katz, D. and Kahn, R.L. (1966). *The Social Psychology of Organizations,* New York: John Wiley.

Keeley, M. (1978). A Social Justice Approach to Organizational Evaluation. *Administrative Science Quarterly,* 23: 272-92.

Kefalas, A.G. and Schoderbak, P.P. (1973). Scanning the Business Environment: Some Empirical Results. *Decision Sciences,* 4: 63-74.

Kegan, R. (1982). *The Evolving Self.* Cambridge, MA: Harvard University Press.

Kerr, N. and Brunn, S. (1981). Ringelman Revisited: Alternative Explanations for Social Loafing Effect. *Personality and Social Psychology Bulletin,* 7: 224-31.

————(1983). The Dispensability of Member Effort and Group Motivation Losses: Free-rider Effects. *Journal of Personality and Social Psychology,* 44: 78-94.

Kerr, S., Glinow, M.A.V. and Schriesheim, J. (1977). Issues in the Study of 'Professionals' in Organizations: The Case of Scientists and Engineers. *Organizational Behavior and Human Performance,* 18:. 329-45.

Kets de Vries, M. and Miller, D. (1984) *The Neurotic Organization.* San Francisco: Jossey-Bass.

Khandwalla, P.N. (1972). Environment and its Impact on the Organization. *International Studies of Management and Organization,* 2: 297-313.

————(1973). Viable and Effective Organizational Designs of Firms. *Academy of Management Journal,* 16: 481-95.

————(1977). *The Design of Organizations.* New York: Harcourt Brace, Jovanovich.

————(1981). Strategy for Turning Around Complex Sick Organizations. *Vikalpa,* 6: 143-66.

————(1982). Some Lessons for the Management of Public Enterprises. *Vikalpa,* 7: 311-26.

————(1983). P I Management. *Vikalpa,* 8: 220-38.

————(1984). *Fourth Eye: Excellence Through Creativity.* Allahabad: A.H. Wheeler.

————(1988). Organizational Effectiveness, In J. Pandey (Ed.), *Psychology in India: The State of the Art* (Vol. III). *Organizational Behavior and Mental Health.* New Delhi: Sage, 197-215.

Khandwalla, P.N. and Jain, G.R. (1984). Organizational Goals and Lower Management Job Satisfaction. *Indian Journal of Industrial Relations*, 20: 111-136.

Khanna, I. and Subramanian, A. (1982). Lesson from Antyodaya for Integrated Rural Development. *Vikalpa*, 7: 227-34.

Khurana, R. (1981). *Growth of Large Businesses: Impact of Monopolies Legislation*, New Delhi: Wiley Eastern.

Kim, L. (1980). Organizational Innovation and Structure. *Journal of Business Research*, 225-45.

Kimberly, J.R. and Rottman, D.B. (1987). Environment, Organization and Effectiveness: A Biographical Approach. *Journal of Management Studies*, 24(6): 595-622.

Klemp, G.O., and McClelland, D.C. (1986) What Characterizes Intelligent Functioning among Senior Managers. In R.J. Sternberg and R.K. Wagner (Eds.). *Practical Intelligence: Nature and Origins of Competence in the Everyday World*. Cambridge, MA: Cambridge University Press.

Knapp, R. (1962). Changing Functions of the College Professor. In N. Sanford (Ed.) *The American College*. New York: John Wiley.

Knasel, E.G., Super, D.E. and Kidd, J.M. (1981). *Work Salience and Work Values: Their Dimensions Assessment and Significance*. National Institute for Career Education and Counselling, Bayfordbury Brouse, USA.

Knowles, M.C. and Taylor, D. (1990). Conceptualizations of Work, Family and Leisure by Managers of Information Technology. *International Journal of Psychology*, 25: 735-50.

Kogan, N. and Wallach, M.A. (1964). *Risk-taking: A Study in Cognition and Personality*. New York: Holt, Rinehart and Winston.

Kohlberg, L. (1969). Stage and Sequence: The Cognitive and Developmental Approach to Socialization Theory and Research. In D.A. Goslin (Ed.), *Handbook of Socialization Theory and Research*. Chicago: Rand-McNally.

Kohn, M.L. (1976). Occupational structure and alienation. *American Journal of Sociology*, 82: 111-67.

Kotter, J.P. (1982). What Effective General Managers Really Do? *Harvard Business Review*, 60(6): 156-67.

Kouzes, J.M. and Posner, B.Z. (1988). *The Leadership Challenge: How to Get Extraordinary Things Done in Organizations*. San Francisco: Jossey-Bass.

Kravitz, D.A. and Waller, J.E. (1980). Effects of Task Interest and Competition on Social Loafing, Paper presented at the Academy of Management, Anaheim, CA.

Krishna Kumar (1982). *Organization and Ownership: A Comprative Sectoral Study of General Management Functions*, New Delhi: Macmillan.

Krishnaswamy, K.S. (1980). What Ails the Public Sector? *Reserve Bank of India Bulletin*, 969-79.

Kurke, L.B. and Aldrich, H.E. (1979). Mintzberg was Right: A Replication and Extension of the Nature of Managerial Work. Paper presented at the Annual meeting of the Academy of Management, Atlanta: GA..

Lakein, A. (1973). *How to Get Control of Your Time and Your Life?* New York: The New American Library.

Langer, E.J. and Benevento, A. (1978). Self-induced Dependence. *Journal of Personality and Social Psychology*, 36: 886-93.

Latham, G.P. and Locke, E.A. (1979). Goal setting—A Motivational Technique that Works. *Organizational Dynamics*, 68-80.

Lawrence, P.R. and Lorsch J. (1967). *Orgazination and Environment,* Boston: Harvard University Press.

Leavitt, H.J. (1975). Beyond the Analytic Manager (Part 2). *California Management Review*, 67: 4.

Lefcourt, H.M. (1978). *Locus of Control: Current Trends in Theory and Research.* Hillsdale, N.J.: Lawrence Erlbaum Associates.

Levinson, H. (1980). Criteria for Choosing Chief Executives. *Harvard Business Review*, 58(4): 113-20.

Levi-Strauss, Claude. (1963). *Structural Anthropology.* New York: Basic Books.

Lewin, K. (1951). *Field Theory in Social Science,* New York: Harper & Row.

Lewin, A.Y. and Minton, J.W. (1986). Determining Organizational Effectiveness: Another Look and an Agenda for Research. *Management Science*, 32(5): 514-38.

Locke, E.A. (1968). Toward a Theory of Task Motivation and Incentives. *Organizational Behavior and Human Performance*, 3: 157-89.

Locke, E.A. and Latham, G.P. (1990). *A Theory of Goal setting and Task Performance,* Englewood Cliffs, NJ: Prentice-Hall.

Loevinger, J. (1976). *Ego Development: Conception and Theories.* San Francisco: Jossey-Bass.

Longman, D.G. and Atkinson, R.H. (1988). *College Learning and Study Skills,* St. Paul, MN: West Publishing Co.

Lyons, T. (1971). Role Clarity, Need for Clarity, Satisfaction, Tension and Withdrawal. *Organizational Behavior and Human Performance*, 6, 99-110.

Macan, T.H., Shahani, C., Dipboye, R.L. and Phillips, A.P. (1990). College Students' Time Management: Correlations with Academic Performance and Stress. *Journal of Educational Psychology*, 82, 4, 760-68.

Mackenzie, K.D. (1986). Virtual Positions. *Management Science*, 32, 622-42.

Madison, D.L., Allen, R.W., Porter, L.W. Renwick, P.A. and Mays, B.T. (1980). Organizational Politics: An Exploration of Managers' Perceptions. *Human Relations*, 33: 79-100.

Maheshwari, B.L. and Malhotra, A.K. (1977). Structural Changes in Indian Companies. In D.P. Sinha (Ed.) Readings in Organization Behaviour (mimeo) Hyderabad: ASCI.

Maier, S.F. and Seligman, M.E.P. (1976). Learned Helplessness: Theory and Evidence. *Journal of Experimental Psychology: General* 105: 3-46.

Martin, J., Sitkin, S. and Boehm, M. (1984). Founders and the Elusive Myth of a Cultural Legacy. Paper presented at the meeting of the Academy of Management, Boston, MA.

Mason, R. and Mitroff, I. (1981). *Challenging Strategic Planning Assumptions,* New York: John Wiley.

McCaul, K.D., Hinsz, V.B. and McCaul, H.S. (1987). The Effects of Commitment to Performance Goals on Effort. *Journal of Applied Social Psychology*, 17(5): 437-50.

McClelland, D.C. (1961). *The Achieving Society.* Prenceton, NJ: Van Nostrand.

———(1975). *Power The Inner Experience.* New York: Irvington.

McDonnell, J.F. (1974). The Human Element in Decision-making. *Personal Journal*, 188-90.

Mento, A.J., Locke, E.A. and Klein, H.J. (1992). Relationship of Goal Level to Valence and Instrumentality. *Journal of Applied Psychology*, 77(4): 395-405.

Merron, K., Fisher, D. and Torbert, W.R. (1987). Meaning Making and Management Action. *Group and Organization Studies*, 12(3): 274-86.

Mikulincer, M. (1989). Cognitive Interference and Learned Helplessness: The Effects of Off-Task Cognitions on Performance Following Unsolvable Problems. *Journal of Personality and Social Psychology*, 57: 601-07.

Miles, R.H. (1980). *Macro Organizational Behavior*. Santa Monica, CA: Goodyear.

Miles, R.H. and Cameron, K.S. (1982) *Coffin Nails and Corporate Strategies*. Englewood Cliffs, NJ: Prentice Hall.

Miles, R.H. and Snow, C. (1978). *Organizational Strategy, Structure and Process*, New York: McGraw-Hill.

Miller, D. and Droge, C. (1986). Psychological and traditional determinants of structure. *Administrative Science Quarterly*, 31: 539-60.

Miller, D. and Friesen, P.H. (1983). Strategy Making and Environment: The Third Link. *Strategic Management Journal*, 5: 221-35.

———(1984) *Organizations: A Quantum view*. Englewood Cliffs, NJ: Prentice Hall.

Miller, D., Kets de Vries, M.F.R. and Toulouse, J. (1982). Top Executive Locus of Control, and its Relationsship to Strategy-making, Structure and Environment. *Academy of Management Journal*, 25(2): 237-53.

Miller, D., Toulouse, Jean-Marie and Belanger, N. (1985). Top Executive Personality and Corporate Strategy: Three Tentative types. In R. Lamb and P. Shrivastava (Ed.) *Advances in Strategic Management*, 4: 223-32. Greenwich, CT: Jai Press Inc.

Miller, D. and Toulouse, Jean-Marie (1986). Chief Executive Personality and Corporate Strategy and Structure in Small Firms. *Management Science*, 32: 1389-1409.

Miner, J.B. (1978). *The Management Process:* New York: MacMillan.

Mintzberg, H. (1973). *The Nature of Management Work*. New York: Harper & Row.

———(1978). Patterns in Strategy Formation. *Management Science*, 24(9): 934-48.

———(1979). *The Structuring of Organizations: A Synthesis of Research*. Englewood Cliffs, NJ: Prentice Hall.

———(1987). The Strategy Concept: Five Ps for Strategy. *California Management Review*, 30: 11-24.

———(1991). The Effective Organization: Forces and Forms. *Sloan Management Review*, 54-67.

Mishra, R. (1982). Some Determinants of Organizational Effectiveness. *Productivity*, 23: 275-85.

Mitchell, T.R., (1975). Expectancy Models of Job Satisfaction, Occupational Preference and Effort: A Theoretical, Methodological and Empirical Appraisal. *Psychological Bulletin*, 81: 1053-77.

Mitchell, T.R., Symser, C.M. and Weed, S.E. (1975). Locus of Control: Supervision and Work Satisfaction. *Academy of Management Journal*, 18: 623-31.

Mitchell, T.R., Rediker, K. and Beach. L. (1986). Image Theory and Organizational

Decision-making. In H. Sims and D. Gioia (Eds.) *The Thinking Organization*, San Francisco: Jossey-Bass.

Mohr, L.B. (1983). The Implications of Effectiveness Theory for Managerial Practice in the Public Sector. In K.S. Cameron and D.A. Whetten: *Organizational Effectiveness: A Comparison of Multiple Models.* New York: Academic Press.

Molnar, J.J. and Rogers, D.L. (1976). Organizational Effectiveness: An Empirical Comparison of the Goal and System Resource Approaches. *The Sociological Quarterly,* 17: 401-13.

Morse, J. and Wagner, F.R. (1978). Measuring the Process of Managerial Effectiveness. *Academy of Management Journal,* 21(1): 23-35.

Mossholder, K.W., Bedeian, A.G. and Armenakiss, A.A. (1981). Role Perceptions, Satisfaction and Performance: Moderating Effects of Self-esteem and Organizational Level. *Organizational Behavior and Human Performance,* 28: 224-34.

Mott, P.E. (1972). *The Characteristics of Effective Organizations.* New York: Harper & Row.

Murdia, R. (1978). Task Structure and Management Processes in Human Services Organizations. *Indian Journal of Social Work,* 39: 273-88.

Murthy, K.R.S. (1982). Top Management Selection for Public Enterprises: Is Private Sector Model Appropriate? *Vikalpa,,* 7: 9-18.

Myrdal, G. (1968). *Asian Drama.* London: Penguin.

Narain, L. (1981). Organizational Structure in Large Public Enterprises: Case Studies of Five Major Public Enterprises. New Delhi: Ajanta.

Naylor, J.C. and Ilgen, D.R. (1984). Goal Setting: A Theoretical Analysis of a Motivational Technology. *Research in Organizational Behavior,* 6: 95-140.

Niehoff, B.P., Enz, C.A. and Grover, R.A. (1990). The Impact of Top Management Actions on Employee Attitudes and Perceptions. *Group and Organization Studies,* 15(3): 337-52.

Organ, D.W. and Greene, C.N. (1974). Role Ambiguity, Locus of Control and Work Satisfaction. *Journal of Applied Psychology*, 59: 101-107.

Orpen, C. (1978). Interpersonal Communication Processes as Determinants of Employee Perceptions of Organizational Goals. *Management and Labor Studies,* 4: 50-88.

Padaki, R. (1984). How Enriched is your Job? *Journal of the Textile Association* 45: 54-62.

Patil, S.M. (1981). Experiences of a Public Sector Top Executive: Handicaps, Disappointments and Fulfilments of a Public Sector Chief. Paper released by the Documentation Centre for Corporate and Business Policy Research, New Delhi.

Paul, O. (1983). Government–Business Interface. *Abhigyan,* Spring, 72-84.

Pavett, C.M. and Lau, A.W. (1983). Managerial Work: The Influence of Hierarchical Level and Functional Speciality. *Academy of Management Journal,* 26(1): 170-77.

Pendse, U. (1983). Evolution of Management Systems in Two Indian Business Groups. Unpublished doctoral dissertation, Indian Institute of Management, Ahmedabad.

Penley, L.E., Alexander, E.R., Jernigan, I.E. and Henwood, C.I (1991) Communication Abilities of Managers: The Relationship to Performance. *Journal of Management,* 17: 57-76.

Pennings, J.M. and Goodman, P.S. (1977). Toward a Workable Framework. In Goodman, P.S. et al. *New Perspectives in Organizational Effectiveness.* San Francisco: Jossey-Bass.

Perrow, C. (1972). *Complex Organizations: A Critical Essay.* New York: Scott Foresman.

Peters, T.J. and Waterman, R.H. (1982). *In Search of Excellence: Lessons from America's Best Run Companies.* New York: Harper & Row.

Pfeffer, J. and Salancik, G.R. (1978). *The External Control of Organizations: A Resource Dependence Perspective.* New York: Harper & Row.

Phares, E.J. (1976). *Locus of Control in Personality.* Morristown, N.J.: General Learning Press.

Porter, M.E. (1980). *Competitive Strategy.* New York: The Free Press.

————(1985) *Competitive Advantage.* New York: The Free Press.

Porter, L.W., Allen, R.W. and Angle, H.L. (1981). The Politics of Upward Influence in Organizations. In B.M. Staw and L.L. Cummings (Eds.). *Research in Organizational Behavior* (Vol. 3). Greenwich, CT: Jai Press Inc.

Porter, L.W. and Lawler, E.E. (1968). *Managerial Attitudes and Performance.* Homewood, IL: Dorsey.

Prahlad, C.K. and Thomas, P.S. (1977). Turnaround Strategy: Lessons from HPF's Experience. *Vikalpa* 2: 99-112.

Price, J.L. (1972). Study of Organizational Effectiveness. *Sociological Quarterly,* 13:3-15.

Pryer, M.W. and Distefano, M.K. Jr. (1971). Perception of Leadership Behavior, Job satisfaction and Internal-external Control across Three Nursing Levels. *Nursing Research,* 20: 534-37.

Pugh, D.S., Hickson, D.J., Hinings, C.R. and Turner, C. (1968) Dimensions of Organizational Structure. *Administrative Science Quarterly.* 13: 65-105.

————(1969) The Context of Organizational Structures. *Administrative Science Quarterly,* 14: 91-114.

Quinn, J.G. (1980). *Strategies for Change.* Homewood, IL.: Irwin.

Quinn, R. and McGrath, M.R. (1984). Applying the Competing Values Approach to the study of Organizational Culture and Effectiveness. Paper presented at the meeting of the Academy of Management. Boston, MA.

Quinn, R.E. and Rohrbaugh, J. (1983). A Spatial Model of Effectiveness Criteria: Towards a Competing Values Approach to Organizational Analysis. *Management Science,* 29: 363-77.

Ramamurthi, R. (1982). Strategic behavior and effectiveness of state owned enterprises in high technology industries: A comparative study in the heavy engineering industry in India. Unpublished doctoral dissertation, Harvard Business School, Boston.

Ranson, S., Hinnings, B. and Greenwood, R. (1980). The Structuring of Organizational Structures. *Administrative Science Quarterly,* 25: 1-17.

Reichers, A.E. (1985). A Review and Reconceptualization of Organizational Commitment. *Academy of Management Review,* 10: 465-76.

Ring, P.S. and Perry, J.L. (1985). Strategic Management in Public and Private

Organizations: Implications of Distinctive Contexts and Constraints. *Academy of Management Review,* 10 (2): 276-80.

Rotter, J.B. (1966). Generalized Expectancies for Internal versus External Control of Reinforcement. *Psychological Monographs: General and Applied,* (80, Whole no. 609).

Roy, S.K. (1974). *Corporate Issues in India.* New Delhi: SRCIR & HR.

Rumelt, R.P. (1974). *Strategy, Structure and Economic Performance.* Boston: Harvard University Press.

Sachdev, A., Pande, S. and Easwaram, J. (1986). Managerial Accountability: Authority and Effectiveness. Paper Presented for 12th National Competition for Young Managers (mimeo).

Salancik, G.R. (1977). Commitment and the Control of Organizational Behavior and Belief. In Barry M Staw and G.R. Salancik (Eds.) *New directions in Organizational Behavior.* Chicago: St. Clair, pp. 1-53.

Satow, R.L. (1975). Value Rational Authority and Professional Organizations: Weber's Missing Type. *Administrative Science Quarterly,* 20: 526-31.

Satyanand, K. (1984). Profile of the Indian Directior: Some Related Issues. *Abhigyan,* Spring, 32-38.

Schall, M. (1983). A Communication-rules Approach to Organizational Culture. *Administrative Science Quarterly,* 28(4): 557-81.

Schmidt, F., Hunter, J., McKenzie, R. and Muldrow, T. (1979). Impact of Valid Selection Procedures on Work-force Productivity *Journal of Applied Psychology,* 64: 609-26.

Schnake, M.E. (1991). Equity in Effort: The 'Sucker Effect' in Coacting Groups. *Journal of Management,* 17(1): 41-55.

Schon, D.A. (1983): *The Reflective Practitioner.* New York: Basic Books.

Schuler, R.S. (1975). Role Perceptions, Satisfaction and Performance: A Partial Reconciliation. *Journal of Applied Psychology,* 60: 683-87.

Scott, B.R. (1977). Effectiveness of Organizational Effectiveness Studies. In P.S. Goodman and J.M. Pennings (Eds.). *New Perspectives on Organizational Effectiveness.* San Francisco, Calif.: Jossey-Bass, pp. 63-95.

Seashore, S.E. (1979). Assessing Organizational Effectiveness with Reference to Member Needs. Paper presented at the meeting of the Academy of Management, Atlanta, GA.

Seeman, M. (1967). On the Personal Consequences of Alienation in Work. *American Sociological Review,* 32: 273-85.

Selman, R.L. (1980). *The Growth of Interpersonal Understanding.* New York: Academic Press.

Shapero, A. (1975). The Displaced, Uncomfortable Entrepreneur. *Psychology Today,* November: 83-86.

Shapira, Z. and Dunbar, R. (1980). Testing Mintzberg's managerial roles classification using in-basket simulation. *Journal of Applied Psychology,* 65(1): 87-95.

Singh, J. (1978). Toward a General Concept of Organizational Effectiveness. *Management and Labor Studies,* 4: 124-33.

———(1985). Technology Size and Organizational Structure: A Re-examination of the Okayama Data. Working paper, Faculty of Management Studies, University of Toronto.

Singh, N.K., Kaul, R. and Ahluwalia, P. (1983). A Diagnostic Study of Training and Development Needs in a Public Sector Organization (mimeo) New Delhi: FORE.

Singh, N.K. and Paul, O. (1985). *Corporate Soul: Dynamics of Effective Management.* New Delhi: Vikas Publ. House Pvt. Ltd.

Singh, P. and Pant, K. (1982). Public Enterprises in India: A case of Managerial Helplessness. *Indian Journal of Industrial Relations,* 18: 175-93.

Singhal, S. (1982). Personal and Perceived Environmental Correlates of Uncertainty: A Micro Study of Small-scale Entrepreneurs in India. *Journal of Economic Psychology,* 2: 115-23.

Sinha, J.B.P. (1973). *Some Problems of Public Sector Organizations.* New Delhi: National Publishing House.

————(1980). *The Nurturant Task Leader.* New Delhi: Concept.

————(1988). *Work Culture in Indian Organizations* (mimeo). Based or ICSSR Research Project, Socio-technical determinants of work values.

Sorenson, J.E. and Sorenson, T.L. (1974). The Conflict of professionals in Bureaucratic Organizations. *Administrative Science Quarterly,* 19: 98-105.

Spector, P.E. (1982). Behavior in Organizations as a Function of Employees' Locus of Control. *Psychological Bulletin,* 91(3): 482-97.

Spybey, T. (1984). Frames of Meaning: The Rationality in Organizational Cultures. *Acta Sociologica,* 27(4): 311-22.

Stebbins, R.A. (1970). On Misunderstanding the Concept of Commitment: A Theoretical Clarification. *Social Forces,* 48: 526-29.

Steers, Richard M. (1975). Problems in the Measurement of Organizational Effectiveness. *Administrative Science Quarterly,* 20: 546-58.

Stevens, J.M., Beyer, J.M. and Trice, H.M. (1978). Assessing Personal, Role and Organizational Predictors of Managerial commitment. *Academy of Management Journal,* 21: 380-96.

Sutton, R.I. and Kahn R.L. (1987). Prediction, Understanding and Control as Antidotes to Organizational Stress. In Lorsch, J.W. (Ed.) *Handbook of Organizational Behavior,* Englewood Cliffs, NJ: Prentice Hall.

Szilagyi, A. (1977). An Empirical Test of Causal Inference between Role Perceptions, Satisfaction with Work, Performance and Organizational level. *Personnel Psychology,* 30: 375-88.

Szilagyi, A., Sims, H. and Keller, R. (1976). Role Dynamics, Locus of Control, and Employee Attitudes and Behavior. *Academy of Management Journal,* 19: 259-76.

Thompson, J.D. (1967). *Organizations in Action.* New York: McGraw-Hill.

Tsui, A.S., and Ohlott, P. (1988). Multiple Assessment of Managerial Effectiveness: Inter Rater Agreement and Consensus in Effectiveness Models. *Personnel Psychology,* 41: 779-803.

Tushman, M.L. and Morse, W. (1982). *Reading in the Management of Innovation.* Boston: Pitman.

Van de Ven, A. and Ferry, D. (1980). *Measuring and Assessing Organizations.* New York: Wiley Inter Science.

Vollmer, H.M. and Mills, D.L. (1966). *Professionalization.* Englewood Cliffs, N.J.: Prentice Hall.

Wagner, R.K. and Sternberg, R.J. (1986). Tacit Knowledge and Intelligence in the Everyday World. In R.J. Sternberg and R.K. Wagner (Eds.) *Practical Intelligence: Nature and Origins of competence in the Everyday World.* Cambridge, MA: Cambridge University Press.

Warner, W.K. (1967). Problems in Measuring the Goals of Voluntary Associations. *Journal of Adult Education,* 19: 3-14.

Willard, Gary E. and Cooper, A.C. (1985). Survivors of Industry Shakeouts: The Case of the US Color Television Set Industry. *Strategic Management Journal,* 6: 299-318.

Willer, C.R. and Henderson, L.S. (1988). Traditional Managers vs Communication Competence Behaviors: An Exploratory Study. Paper presented at the Academy of Management. Anaheim, CA.

Wolfe, R.N. (1972). Effects of Economic Threat on Autonomy and Perceived Locus of Control. *The Journal of Social Psychology,* 86: 233-40.

Wolfe, R.N. and Grosch, J.W. (1990). Personality Correlates of Confidence in One's Decisions. *Journal of Personality,* 58(3): 515-34.

Yuchtman, E. and Seashore, S.E. (1967). A systems Resource Approach to Organizational Effectiveness. *American Sociological Review,* 32: 891-903.

Zahra, S.A. (1984). Antecedents and Consequences of Organizational Commitment: An Integrative Approach. *Akron Business and Economic Review,* 15: 26-32.

Zammuto, R.F. (1982). *Assessing Organizational Effectiveness.* Albany: State University of New York Press.

INDEX

access, managers', to structures and products, 58
accountability, 170
appraising role, of managers, 101
attitudinal interventions, 84
attitudinal outcomes, 104
authority, delegation of, 169
autonomy, for public sectors, 60, 154

basic industries, 30
Bharat Heavy Electricals Ltd. (BHEL), 33
boards, *see* management boards
Bureau of Public Enterprises, 29, 35
bureaucracy, 22, 33, 162
bureaucratized orientation, in public sectors, 59

chief executive's jobs, 165
clarity in role performance, 103, 104, 105, 106, 107, 108, 109, 110, 112, 117, 122, 174, 175, 176
Company Law Board, 158
communication, 112, 136; gap, 119; inadequate, 164; skills, 155
competitiveness, 32, 148
composite trends, 94–98; and directions, 113–17; and professional commitment, 142–48
conceptual model, of management, 40, 181
confidence, of managers, 118ff, 175, 176
confidential reports, 169
congruence theory, 62
contingency behaviour theory, of organizational effectiveness, 17

contingency theorists, 49
control, locus of, 42, 43, 44, 50, 58, 62, 68
coordinating role, of managers, 101
core group, 13
corporate culture, 161–64, 177
corporate goals, 13, 14, 36, 37; *see also,* goals
corporate management, issues in, 28ff
corporate set-up, in India, 29–30
'corporate soul', 24
corruption, 176
cost overruns, 70

decision-making, by managers, 18, 19, 36, 37, 38, 44, 45, 62, 64, 165, 166, 169–70
developing countries, functions of management in, 14
developmental approach, to individual differences, 19–21
differentiation aspect, of structure, 50, 51, 54, 93, 97, 116, 141, 142, 146, 149; and confidence of managers, 125, 126, 130, 131; and time spent, 81
disciplinary process, 168
discussions, time spent on, with juniors, 77–78, 79, 125, 139, 140; with superiors, 74, 75, 80, 81, 109, 124, 130, 131, 132, 139, 174
dynamism of environment, 141, 175; heterogeneity and, 64

'ecology model', 16
effective managers, 23–26
effectiveness, causality of, 17

employee commitment, 112; *see also*, professional commitment
employee loyalty, 17
environment, dynamism in, 65, 93, 97, 141, 175; dynamism in, role perception, 112, 116; dynamism of, and confidence of managers, 126, 131; dynamism of, and time spent on inspection, 80, 81; external, 158–59; heterogeneity in, 63, 64, 65, 94, 141, 142, 144, 145, 175; heterogeneity in, and confidence of managers, 131; heterogeneity in, and time spent, 81; perceptions of, 39, 42, 47–49; strategy-making, structure and, 51–53, 63–65, 109–13; strategy-making, structure and, and confidence of managers, 125–27; strategy-making, structure, personal orientation and, 53–62, 91–94; strategy-making, structure and, professional commitment, 140–42, 143, 144, 145, 149; strategy-making, structure and, and variables of time, 79–81; turbulence in, 66–67
equity, and social justice, 177
evaluation, 86
executive leadership, 17
externality-oriented managers (externals), level of confidence in, 122; role perception of, 108, 113, 116; time spent by, 77, 78, 79, 81; variables of confidence in, 124, 125, 126, 130; variables of goal achievement for, 97; variables for professional commitment in, 146, 147, 149

family-related activities, time spent on, 70, 71, 72, 80, 82
feedback system, 133; inadequate, 164
futurity strategy, 47, 54, 55, 58, 63, 65, 79, 138, 174, 175; and confidence of managers, 125, 126, 130; goal achievement and, 91, 92, 93; and professional commitment, 140, 141, 142, 144, 145, 146, 149; and role perception, 109, 112, 116

globalization, 32

goal, and action management, 102; achievement, 85ff, 132, 174, 175, 176; achievement, concept and measure of, 87–88; achievement, confidence of managers and, 122; achievement, and time management, 89–91, 94–97; approach, to individual differences, 19; model, 15; theory, 86
governance, 'soft' system of, 73
government, public sector's dependence on, 36; control over public sector, 62, 76, 132, 164, 166, 170, 176; policies of, 156–58
growth and turnaround strategies, 45, 50

helpless managers, 118
hierarchical approach, to individual differences, 22–23
human development, stages of, 20
human relations, 166
human resources management, 17, 102, 171, 179

individual difference dimension, 18–23, 26
individual goals, 85, 86
Industrial Policy Document of 1980, 31
Industrial Policy Resolutions, 29
Industrial Policy Settlement of Government of India (1948), 29
industrial relations, 35, 66
inferences, and confidence of managers, 131–33; and directions, 82–84
information, attributes of, processing and decision-making, 17; role of managers, 18; system, 178
innovation strategy, 45, 46, 47, 51, 59, 60, 61, 63, 64, 66, 67, 80, 93, 174; and confidence of managers, 130, 132; and professional commitment, 146; and role perception, 110, 112, 116
inspection rounds, 74, 75, 79, 80, 81, 125
institution-building, 155
integrative approach, to individual difference, 23
internality-oriented managers (internals), 43, 44, 55, 58, 59, 60, 61, 93, 175–76; dependent variables of confidence in,

124, 125, 126, 129; dependent variables for goal achievement in, 96; dependent variables for professional commitment in, 146, 147, 149; level of confidence in, 122; role perception of, 108, 110, 111, 113, 115; time spent by, 77, 78, 81

interpersonal role, of managers, 18, 108

labour, legislations, 38, 157; unions and management, 38, 158–59

leadership, 23, 98, 102, 164–68; *see also,* executive leadership

legitimacy model, 15

liberalization, of policies, 31, 180

licensing and regulation policies, 158, 180

life cycle stage, 17

loss-making corporations, analysis of interview responses for, 153; confidence level of managers in, 122; dependent variable of confidence in managers in, 124, 125, 126, 128; dependent variables for goal achievement in, 96; dependent variables for professional commitment in, 146; dependent variables for role perception in, 114; dependent variables for strategy, environment and structure in, 55, 57; innovation strategy in, 64; time spent by managers in, 76, 81

loyalty, 166

maintenance model, 15

management, –employee relations, 155; functions of, 14–15, 112

management boards/board of directors, ineffectiveness of, 159–60

managers (managerial), as bureaucrats, 75; confidence level of, 121–23; contingencies, 42; and effectiveness, 13ff, 156; functions, 121; goals of, 85–88; roles, 18, 22–23, 101, 105–7, 167; and time, 69–70

market trends, time spent on studying, 74, 75, 81, 109, 125, 139

Maruti Udyog Ltd., 34

Memorandum of Understanding (MoU), 34, 159, 182

mixed economy model, 182

Monopolies and Restrictive Trade Practices Commission, 158, 176

motivation, 21, 99, 100

New Industrial Policy, 180

operationalization and measure, of confidence, 120–21

organizational culture, 17, 67

organizational designs, 17

organizational effectiveness, 15–17

organizational goal, identification with, 24; *see also,* goal

overmanning, 170–71, 177; ill-effects of, 83

paperwork, time spent on, 74, 75, 81, 97, 140, 174

perceived control, and actual performance, 118ff

personal care, time spent on, 79, 80

personal commitment, 100, 117, 125, 216

personal orientation, of managers, 39, 42–44, 47, 58, 60, 108, 172, 175, 176; and professional commitment, 143, 145; strategy-making, environment, structure and, 53–62, 91–94; and time management and distribution, 77–79

personality, cult, 164; dispositions, 111; role of, in perception, 111

personnel policies, social welfare and, 171

placement, 171

planning, function, 47; lack of coordination in, 164; and management activity, 116, 125, 139, 140; process, 154; time spent on, 176

policy implications, 179

politicization, of corporations, 161, 162

private sector, analysis of interview responses for, 152; confidence level of managers in, 122; dependent variables of confidence in managers in, 124, 125, 128; dependent variables for goal achievement in 94; dependent variables for role perception in, 113

proactive strategies, 45, 46, 58, 59, 63, 80,